TOO HOT TO HIDE

Remarkable Women Of Fort Lauderdale

by Mae K. Silver

Of the 2012 limited printing of 200, this keepsake copy is_____.

Dedicated to women of
Fort Lauderdale
who still remain hidden
in history.

ISBN: 0-9669913-6-2

Copyright © 2012 Mae K. Silver

Book design, layout, indexing: Chris Carlsson

COVER IMAGE: Katy Rawls as an aviatrix. Image from the International Swimming Hall of Fame.

BACK COVER IMAGE: Fort Lauderdale beach, from the Fort Lauderdale Historical Society.

All proceeds from the sale of Too Hot to Hide *benefit the scholarship fund of the Fort Lauderdale Woman's Club and/or other organizations devoted to women's history.*

TOO HOT TO HIDE

Remarkable Women Of Fort Lauderdale

Preface

The history of Florida is unique. Some say Florida has no history. However, Florida has a very early white history in that a white Spaniard named Ponce de Leon walked on a land mass in 1513 and named it Florida. No other land in America can make that claim. The English settled Jamestown in 1607, the Pilgrims in 1620. A town in northeast Florida, by the name of St. Augustine, founded by an African-American, had begun decades earlier. However, the confusion is understandable in that the coming of the white Americans to Florida did not begin until the 18th century and accelerated in the 19th. So white American history did not begin until then. That's correct.

Fort Lauderdale is the youngest town I have ever lived in. My hometown of New Brunswick, New Jersey dates before the Revolutionary War. My second hometown of 43 years, San Francisco, began in 1776. Bordentown, New Jersey, where I lived and researched Thomas Paine, was started in 1673 by the Quakers. Fort Lauderdale is only one hundred years old this year 2011. Nevertheless, like any place, it actually does have a history. It is my pleasure to find it and write it.

In my years of researching and writing local history, I decided that women's history is really a code word for......empowerment. So while one can view empowerment mostly as a learned internal psychological state one can also feel empowerment when one reads what women have done that is frequently hidden or obscured. I can remember so vividly that, when I studied one war after another in high school history, I often wondered, "What were women doing at that same time the men were fighting each other?" Fortunately, the women's movement revived itself during the civil rights struggle, and women's history became a separate history to study. Finally, I learned what women did when men went to war in other places.

The title of my book and other historical presentations, "Too Hot to Hide," came from a rather strong suggestion from my daughter who thought I should label my history with some pizzazz. I thought her idea had much credence, particularly, if one thought about Florida and how hot it gets here. But, what should it be? One day while I wandered through the new books section of the main library in Stranahan Park, it came to me in a flash. And it stuck. It is "Too Hot to Hide." It also is the name of my women's history walk in Stranahan Park that I do the first Saturday of each month at 2 pm starting at the Fort Lauderdale Woman's Club. It's also the name of my website.

While some may think that my women's history walk is boring and has no relevance to Fort Lauderdale, I would dispute that. Florida Secretary of State Browning, in his talk to us at the Preservation Conference at the History Commission headquarters on May 26, 2011, gave statistics that state when visitors come to a place for history, they stay 43% longer than others who might come just to find "Mickey or Goofy". This translates into revenue for this town, any town. This also means businesses and jobs can increase when we increase our historical offerings to the tourists. My "Too Hot to Hide" tour, based on a series of paved plaques in Stranahan Park, begun by the Fort Lauderdale Historical Society in 1986, offers yet another way to look at Fort Lauderdale history. When I do it, it is not boring. Come!

Mae Silver

Fort Lauderdale, 2011

Introduction

After I decided which women I would include in my book, it became obvious that to present them in a dictionary way would be rather dull to read. However, more importantly, just a series of biographies would omit for the reader what I had discovered about these women that I found exciting. When one could see how their reactions to events around them pushed them into the actions they took, one could see how they decided to deal with these events. It was and is an historical dance. To present these women and events in a chronological way seemed the best way to show the "dance."

My observation about how history is presented here is that it is often separated. There is white American history. There is African-American history. There is Seminole history. The women I chose for his book are women of all colors because often they worked together about large community issues. In fact, I think it was because of their blended work that very important historic breakthroughs occurred. Therefore, the women I selected were likely to have been the first in their particular endeavor. That meant they often were in the forefront of a larger wave of history that surrounded them. They were trail-blazers.

The most fun I have with history is when I can connect the dots. Large movements or events usually culminated after many little steps occurred earlier. While one often thinks that a powerful event develops overnight, that is only partially so. Early baby steps, repeated many times over have led to that big act. Since women's history is often hidden or obscured, it suggests a route to locate some of those preliminary, almost rehearsal steps that led to the big finale. To dig out women's history is hard work. But even that is fun because it becomes as close to detective work as that shown on television programs. It is not unusual to find that the women who made some of those early steps were still unknown. Annie Reed is one example of a woman who was virtually unknown in either the white or black community. Lorna Simpson and Stella Taylor were two others. I revised the legendary story of Frank Stranahan who sold the property on which Dillard School was built for one dollar. Those dots had not been connected before and when I connected them, a larger, different picture suddenly unfolded. I find that exciting.

In 20th century America, the struggle for individual freedoms regardless of color, gender, and sexual orientation transformed our society and culture. Often these efforts gained credence through federal intervention and legislation. Men and women alike shared the fight. Witness the end of the 41 years of Seminole Wars, the arrival of the railroad, the Seminole acquisition of their reservation, the racial integration of Fort Lauderdale's public school system and other public places, the preservation movement, WWII, the efforts for women's vote and rights, and the transformation of Fort Lauderdale into the Venice of America. In all of these changes, women of all colors left their marks. They were "Too Hot to Hide."

Each of these women's stories could easily have filled its own book. Actually, I have not given them all of what they deserve with these short written versions of their lives. Their passion for excellence in whatever part of life they embraced especially shows in the "Women's Firsts" Roll I created. These women showed a particular talent for finding and defining themselves in their contributions to the place where they lived—Fort Lauderdale. My father taught me a belief. He said, "There is no one right way to do anything. The task is to find your way and do it." Each of these women showed how to do it and will forever serve as an inspiration for each of us women to find our own way in this life in Fort Lauderdale. That is empowerment.

TABLE OF CONTENTS

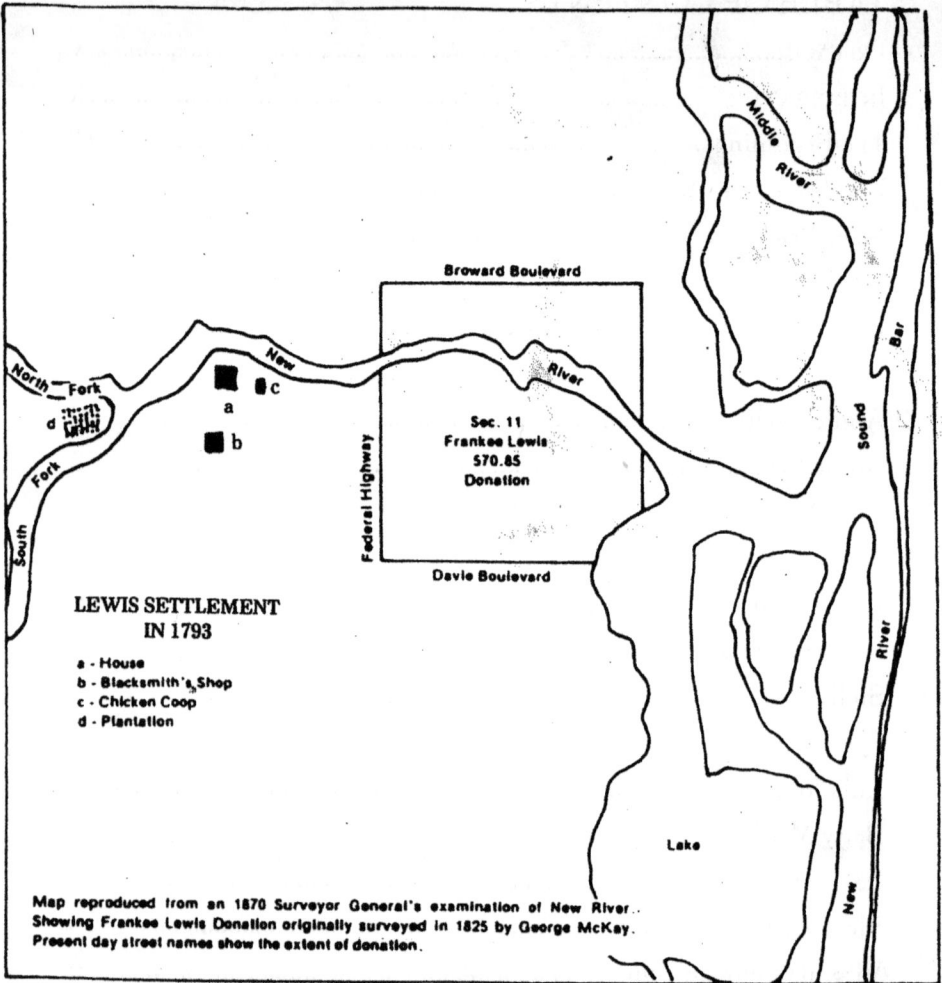

Inside map:

Middle River

North Fork

New River

Broward Boulevard

Sec. 11
Frankee Lewis
570.85
Donation

Federal Highway

Davie Boulevard

South Fork

Sound

Bar

River

LEWIS SETTLEMENT
IN 1793

a - House
b - Blacksmith's Shop
c - Chicken Coop
d - Plantation

Lake

New

Map reproduced from an 1870 Surveyor General's examination of New River.
Showing Frankee Lewis Donation originally surveyed in 1825 by George McKay.
Present day street names show the extent of donation.

Frankee Lewis Donation (1824)
includes property on both sides of the New River.
Source: Broward Legacy, Vol. 13, Summer/Fall, 1990.

The Beginning

The Lewis family, Surles, Frankee, Jonathan, Surles Jr., and William became the first white American family that settled in what became Fort Lauderdale. Their exact arrival, about 1786 or 1787, is not clear. Two other families, named Egan and Pent, were in the Miami River area. The Lewises settled in the area now called Tarpon Bend, perhaps in the area of today's South Andrews Avenue. They were farmers. If they moved here to find peace and tranquility, to rest from their turbulent relocations, maybe that did not happen.

When they arrived, the land belonged to the British. That seemed safe since they were British sympathizers. But unknown to them, British governance would soon be replaced by Spanish. In their flight from one of the American colonies to the Bahamas after the Revolutionary War peace treaty in 1783, they were still, on one level, Americans and not British subjects, even though they were British sympathizers. America still had more wars it would march into. By 1812, the new country was at war again with the British and 1817 saw the beginning of a 41-year war with the Seminoles in Florida. Those repeated wars with the Seminoles would keep other pioneer settlers from joining the Lewises as neighbors. The Lewis Family was alone in their early years from about 1786 to 1825 when other settlers began moving into the area.

The beginnings of the Industrial Revolution showed in other parts of the country: Robert Fulton's steamboat and submarine, gaslights in New York, horse-drawn trolleys, the steam engine and the first railroad. But progress didn't reach Florida. As the Seminole Wars carried on, the news of those wars spread throughout the country and kept most settlers away for years. Growth and prosperity in Florida were postponed, all that time lost as the army fought to capture land for white Americans alone to populate. These were wars with impossible goals.

During the Second Seminole War, the Americans, particularly Congress and the Washingtonians, grew weary and tired of the expense. A scheme developed to defray the cost of the war. Senator Thomas Hart Benton sponsored a bill called the "Army Occupation Act of 1838." This put a different spin on a difficult situation. It was an experiment that could be a win win for all. Florida had lots of land. Why not give land to would-be settlers? However, there was a proviso. The army would no longer be required to protect the settlers. It would help settle folks, but the firearms to protect the settlers were their own responsibility. The Act would support the settlers for one year. Those settlers who left their land previously would be given first priority to file for resettlement.

Floridians, even in the Fort Lauderdale area, benefitted from the Army Occupation Act, along with settlers in the counties of Marion, Hernando, Citrus, Pasco, Polk, Sumnter, Alachwa and Hillsborough. To this day, descendants from these early settlers who became cattle owners can attest to the help their ancestors received from the U.S. government. As a sidebar of information, Abner Doubleday, who was involved in the resettlement, carved a road which today is similar to the route of Federal Highway in Fort Lauderdale. In many ways, the resettlement act alleviated the tension, but not for long. Another war emerged, the Third Seminole War, which historians regard as contrived. Meanwhile, Florida became a state on March 3, 1845.

By this time, people on both sides of the war were really fatigued. The presence of the Seminoles in Florida was minimal. Four days after some of their leaders relented and went west on May 4, 1858, the Third Seminole War officially ended. Or did it? The enduring Seminoles live very well, cared for today by their astonishingly successful Seminole Hard Rock Cafe and Casino on their reservation in Hollywood.

What happened to the Lewis family in light of such turmoil?

Frankee Pickett Lewis (1745-1830)

We know about the Frankee Lewis Donation (1824) which was the American land grant in Fort Lauderdale awarded to Mrs. Lewis but we do not know much about her. She was matriarch of the first white American family that settled in what would eventually be called Fort Lauderdale. Because we do not know much about her, I wanted to find her place in our history.

The story in local history states that Frankee, her husband Surles and their three sons arrived here after 1783 from the Bahamas. They came to the Bahamas, probably Abaco Island, from South Carolina, as part of the

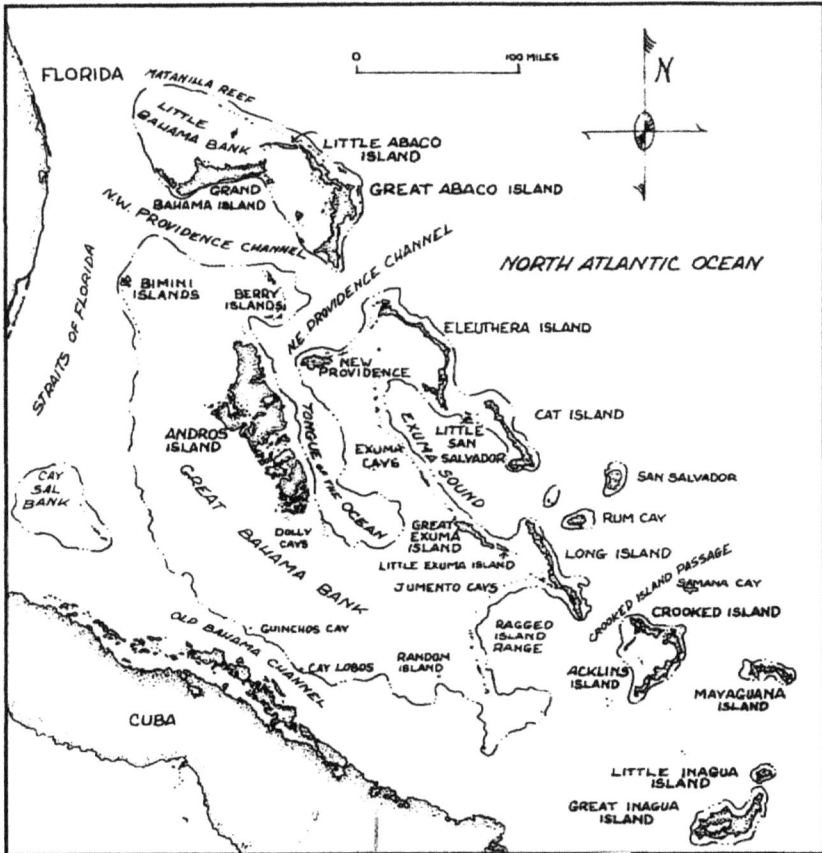

Map of Abaco Islands.

Frankee Lewis image. No known image of Frankee Lewis exists. This by artist Vivian Archer appears in Harold Flagg's article, "Bahamian Lewises: Pioneers of Florida".

mass exodus of loyalists after the Revolutionary War peace treaty was final. It is also not clear as to which island in the Abaco chain the Lewises had settled. Abaco has a land mass of 649 square miles, about half the size of Rhode Island. There are the Great and Little Abaco and smaller cuys that form a chain over 100 miles long. The Abacos lie east of the Bahamas. One assumes loyalists settled in the Great Abaco and founded towns they named Carleton, Marsh's Harbor, Maxwell Town, Spencer's Bight, and Eight Mile Bay. We do not know where the Lewis family settled. We also do not know exactly when they decided to leave Abaco for the east coast of Florida.

The 1783 peace treaty that ended the Revolutionary War made certain stipulations regarding the loyalists and their property. Compensations and judicial redress would give the loyalists an opportunity to reclaim property that had been confiscated during the War. It was an attempt on paper to right the indignities about their property they had suffered as the supporters of the British Monarchy.

The Revolutionary War was actually our first civil war. Imagine living next door to someone who did not support the patriot cause, someone who did not believe in the War, who was not a patriot but a loyalist. In some places people rioted one side against another. Neighbors killed each other, on both sides. Houses were burned, property ravaged, crops stolen. The hazards of one's own neighborhood made living at home as dangerous as being a soldier on the front line. It was a civil war.

Surles owned land in Craven County, South Carolina received as a grant from the British. While Frankee was from Virginia, their family lived in South Carolina in these confusing times during and after the War. The Lewises, like many other farmers, left to find another place not under war. They joined the thousands of loyalists who left their homes in search of land governed by the British. They sought a better life. They were the loyalists who traveled to the Islands.

Records do not clarify with whom the Lewises came. Possibly it was with the group organized by William Augustus Bowles from New York City. This likelihood comes from the fact that they settled in Abaco where the Bowles group landed. At a later time when they owned land in Fort Lauderdale, history states they had horses given to them by Bowles. suggesting a relationship formed at least in Abaco. But other loyalists

The coontie plant. Author's photo.

The Coontie Hatchee Park, 2.64 acres, is at 116 SW 15th Ave. It celebrates that the coontie plant powder was the first industry in southeast Florida. The powder could be used like flour in baking. William Cooley had a successful business here when he milled barrels of the powder and sent them to Key West for further shipping. The plant itself is poisonous. Author's photo.

Too Hot To Hide

departed the U.S. with a British military escort led by Sir Guy Carlton and his associated group from New York City and the Lewises may have been part of that party of 1,458 destined for Abaco. The British promised land to these immigrants. Every head of a family would receive forty acres, and to every white or black man, woman or child in the family, twenty acres, at an annual quit rent of 2s. per hundred acres. Additionally, lands were delivered free of charge and exempted from quit rents for the next ten years. The military in New Providence (Nassau) received provisions for 2,000 men to ease the resettlement of the new populations in the Bahamas. Those islands gained between 6,000 and 7,000 inhabitants of both races from June, 1783 to April, 1785. The islands' population tripled with these new residents. Records are not clear about the number of loyalists who settled in Abaco but the estimate is about 2,000.

A report issued by the British military gave a glowing account of the islands' fertility. It explained the lack of cultivation of the soil was due to the indolence of the resident population. No doubt, continued the report, the soil could support plants grown in the West Indies such as pineapple, oranges, lemons, limes cocoa etc. Little attention was paid to the thin depth of surface soil supported from beneath by its limestone cradle. On Abaco, the Lewises would not have planted cotton but would have tried the vegetable crops they knew from South Carolina. These would have worked up to a point but the soil was not deep enough and could not sustain repeated plantings as theirs had in South Carolina. A hurricane in 1785 certainly increased the difficulty of their experiences in Abaco. Soon they must have realized the promise of fertile agricultural land was only a hope that would never prove true.

The colonization plan of Abaco added to the distress of its new inhabitants. Farms were isolated from each other. The idea to compete with the New England commercial shipping by building ships seemed possible except for the fact that British shipping was not welcomed in those commercial lanes. Also, once ships left Abaco, they rarely returned for there was no cargo in Abaco to load and ship.

Why did the Lewis family choose the Fort Lauderdale area to settle? Perhaps, they learned about the area as land they could farm.

Let us speculate further. Perhaps, they learned that the manico plant that grew in Abaco had a counterpart in the Fort Lauderdale area. One can speculate that they learned how the Lucayans of Abaco transformed the tuberous root of the manico into a white powder from which they made their famous cassava bread. Possibly, they learned that the Native Americans took the coontie root, mashed and mixed it with water and then dried that mixture, which left a residue of a white powder. From that white powder, they made breads etc. That knowledge may have been the decisive factor that made the Lewis family choose the Fort Lauderdale area, where the coontie plant grew in profusion.

One can only imagine how robust and brave the Lewises were to have moved as often as they did before they finally found land where they could cultivate and harvest crops that they could eventually trade. They were farmers first and last, and their market was the Bahamas, especially Nassau. It was during one of these trips that a storm arose, and in it Mr. Lewis and one son drowned. Frankee Lewis became a widow in 1819 but continued to farm and trade as a living. She was no longer living in a land of tranquility. As Florida's three Seminole Wars (1817-1858) raged around her little farm, one wonders how she managed. History makes no note of any problems she may have had with the Seminoles. She lived through British Florida, then Spanish Florida, then American Florida, and she applied for a land grant from the American government. In 1824, she received that grant and it became known as the Frankee Lewis Donation. Its land mass was one acre for her, another for her son Jonathan, and another for her daughter-in-law. After she sold her Donation in 1825 to Richard Fitzpatrick, she moved to be with her son Jonathan in Key West ,where she died in 1830.

Because of a rumor that the Lewis family had connections with William Augustus Bowles, a renegade character potentially problematic to the Spaniards, a Spanish "spy" ship arrived at the Lewis place to investigate their involvement with Bowles. Luckily, the Lewis family was absent on a trading trip to the Bahamas. What the Spaniards observed and reported gave us a picture of the Lewis farm. Englishman Joseph Robbins, with his wife Rachael and daughter Susannah, had remained to care for the Lewis farm while they were away. Also living on the farm was a young American man called Joel Radcliffe. The 1793 report stated that the farm consisted of a small house, barn, chicken coop, blacksmith shop and plantation. It also listed the plants in their garden: pineapples, lemons, oranges, limes, coconuts, sugar apples and guavas. Robbins confirmed the

Bowles connection with the Lewis family in that he had given them five horses. The Spaniards left the Lewis family alone. They seemed satisfied that the Bowles connection posed no threat to them and instead focused on finding Bowles. Eventually they captured him and incarcerated him in the infamous Morro Castle, where he died.

Neither Frankee nor the Lewis family left us records, diaries, or letters about their life. Jonathan's records speak about lands he owned. We do know they were farmers seemingly always looking for good land once they left the colonies. They were hardy people, by definition, to have weathered all these moves in times that were perilous, unpredictable and dangerous. They were our pioneer white American family and Frankee was their mother.

Others began to come, but only after another war, the Civil War, resolved. William and Mary Brickell arrived in Miami in 1871. Along with Julia Tuttle, they gave land to Henry Flagler to entice him to stretch his railroad to Miami. Because they had land in Fort Lauderdale, it was mainly Mary Brickell who convinced Flagler to create a railroad stop in Fort Lauderdale. The arrival of the railroad here made all the difference in the business world. As I began my research into the early history of the town, I began to sense that the Brickells were unsung heroes in bringing the railroad to town in 1896.

I learned that the Brickells in addition to Julia Tuttle, the Mother of Miami, had given Henry Flagler some of their Miami land to lure his railroad to that city. The bronze plaque titled "The Coming of the Railroad in 1896," visible on my walking tour, clearly showed its importance in giving the town a way to ship produce by rail to all parts of the country. In effect, the railroad made Fort Lauderdale a commercial depot and paved way for its economic growth beyond tourism. But the Brickells and particularly Mary gleaned no credit for that crucial happening. When I began my Women's History Walk in Stranahan Park in March 2010, I included Mary Brickell when we looked down at that bronze plaque.

Most recently as I shopped at the Farmer's Market at the Esplanade, I stopped at the Fort Lauderdale Historical Society tent and browsed through their books. Suddenly what popped out at me was a 2011 book titled *William and Mary Brickell* by Beth Brickell. I bought it in a snap. Although I was driving, I literally ran back home and cracked the book. What I discovered validated my hunch about how the Brickells have been omitted from the history of the very important railroad development of Fort Lauderdale.

Mary Bulmer Brickell
(1838-1922)

I n South Florida, streets, parks and islands bear the Brickell name. William and Mary Brickell were pioneers, but pioneers with a sense of vision, intellectual acumen, good business sense and an integrity that was steadfast. While most of their business holdings were in Miami, the Brickells also owned property in Fort Lauderdale, actually 3974 acres on both sides of the New River.[1] It is Mary Brickell who often showed up in early Fort Lauderdale history. She developed subdivisions, Cooley Hammock and Rio Vista, and dedicated roads, thoroughfares and utilities for the public use in perpetuity.[2] Even when she lost

Mary Brickell, FLHS archives.

her lawsuit called *Riparian Rights*, another bronze in the Stranahan Park, her properties then became city property.

When the Brickells moved to Miami, they were already wealthy. While living in Cleveland, Ohio they knew the Rockefellers, Henry Flagler and Julia Tuttle. William had made his fortune by following gold rushes, not only the one in California but also the one in Australia. He was a creative businessman and learned how to turn a dollar into millions. Often William was gone from home in quest of another business venture, and Mary cared for all the children and the property. She proved herself to be a quick learner and showed a visionary flair for turning land into beauty to enhance the people's quality of life. Many examples of this can be seen today in Miami's neighborhoods developed from the Brickell properties.

In the 1870's and '80's, Mary began buying land. By the 1890s, the Brickells owned at least 6,427 acres of prime land in South Florida: 2,000 south of the Miami River, 400 in upper Biscayne Bay, 4,000 at New River (Fort Lauderdale) and 125 in Palm Beach.[3] William had prophesied the coming of the railroad to Miami and that would come in time, he knew. Preparing for another successful business venture, the Brickells bought enough land so they could offer Flagler their acreage to encourage him to bring his railroad to Miami—but also—to Fort Lauderdale. Actually, according to Beth Brickell the Brickells gave more Miami land to Flagler than Julia Tuttle, and they did it earlier than she did. Let's get back to Mary.

Mary and William met in Australia. The Bulmer family arrived in Australia in 1840 from England. Mary was born in Little Bolton, Lancashire, England. Meeting William, she was a dressmaker who soon became pregnant. They did not marry until five years later. They left Australia for New York, then Pittsburgh, then San Francisco. Before settling in San Francisco, they stayed in Washington, D.C, at the time of the Civil War. Mary volunteered as a nurse caring for the critically wounded in Washington. Then they moved to Cleveland, Ohio where Mary had three more children, making a total of six. In Ohio, the Brickells would meet the others who would figure into Florida history: John Rockefeller, Henry Flagler, Ephraim Sturtevant, Julia Tuttle's father. But, Mary did not like the cold weather in Ohio and soon William looked to move to Florida. And so they did, when others saw no reason to go to such a wilderness. The Brickells moved in 1871 to Miami to live among 12 other white families and Seminoles, and became pioneers in paradise. Their business was the Brickell trading post.

Henry Flagler saw little benefit to himself or his business to locate his railroad in Fort Lauderdale. But the Brickells pressed on. He agreed to bring his railroad to where the Brickells indicated, a one-square-mile parcel west of the Frankee Lewis Donation. He built a station there and agreed to develop the town's streets and advertise the city in his promotion of Fort Lauderdale. The Brickells gave him half their land, about 248 acres in town lots plus 21 acres for the railroad right of way. The street building continued in tandem with the railroad construction. The Florida East Coast Railway carried its first passengers into Fort Lauderdale on February 22, 1896, two days after Mary's 60th birthday.[4]

After William's passing in 1908, Mary continued keeping her watchful eye on their properties. She remained actively engaged in what happened. In 1893 when the projected route of the new county road would bisect her New River lands, she requested the county commissioners to move the ferry and

Too Hot To Hide

cut the new county road on the Section Line at New River. Frank Stranahan heard her objection and not only moved his ferry but also his camp about one half mile west along the New River. The commissioners complied with her request but added that she corduroy and bridge the road on the section line. When Frank Stranahan moved his ferry, Mary gave him 300 feet of river frontage as a reward and then he offered to build the bridge which the commissioners refused to do because it was too costly at $500. He asked permission to build the bridge for $45, and the commissioners granted his request. Perhaps, because Frank Stranahan built that bridge, Mary asked him to oversee the Brickell properties in Fort Lauderdale. Additionally, she deeded him 10.7 acres on the New River. In effect, Mary Brickell set him on his way to become the success he became in Fort Lauderdale. The trading post he moved up the river is now the Stranahan House, owned by the Stranahan House and Museum Society.

This vignette reflects the quality of the business relationships that Mary Brickell exercised all her life. She was sometimes called steely-eyed, all business, no nonsense, aloof and not a joiner, but she touched her community wisely when it came to business. Another example of her talent was how she helped other businesses when the dark days of the Panic of 1907 hit Miami and the banks had no cash. Not a believer in banks, Mary had cash available for loans and mortgages during this bleak time. She made business loans and never closed on a mortgage. She conducted business with Native Americans and African Americans but never...never if any of them were drunk. She declared this upfront. In turn, she won their respect.

A very moving article in the *Miami Herald* came from the "Colored People" who mourned her death. It said,

> *"...she helped them in every practicable way to become not only property owners, but better citizens. Her general query to them was not so much 'What have you?' but 'How are you living?'...the colored people of Miami, along with others, will feel her loss keenly."*

Her leadership, vision and plain generosity earned her the admiration of her community even though her eccentric appearance often gave one a second glance. She usually wore a long skirt that ballooned to the ground and dragged on it over her bare feet. She wore no jewelry, just her wedding band. Mary Brickell was a woman of her own definition.

At 86, Mary Brickell died unexpectedly and quickly on Friday morning, January 13,1922 at her home. Her estate valued at five million dollars was left to her six living children.

Frank Stranahan arrived in Fort Lauderdale in 1893. Since he and Mary Brickell were businesspeople, they got to know each other. Mary helped Frank in his early years. Ivy Stranahan, Frank's wife, became an extraordinarily involved social activist who embraced many crucial causes of the times. Her part in Fort Lauderdale history earned her the title Mother of Fort Lauderdale.

Ivy Julia Cromartie Stranahan (1881-1971)

"Watchie-Esta-Hutrie," the Little White Mother, earned her title well from the Seminole people who loved her as much as she loved them. Ivy Stranahan responded to each challenge and problem that came her way. Ninety years of almost non-stop volunteer service on behalf of Fort Lauderdale and particularly its children bound her inextricably with those around her. With no children of her own to tend, she freely "adopted" many children of the Seminole tribe and offered her guidance, education, and direct assistance to those who sought her. So she became their Little White Mother, "Watchie-Esta-Hutrie".

In 1899 Ivy Cromartie came to Fort Lauderdale as its first school teacher. After a year, she and Frank Stranahan married, and their life together filled the pages of Fort Lauderdale's early history. Some say that Fort Lauderdale was founded at Stranahan's trading post. While Frank Stranahan began as a trader, he became a storekeeper, a banker, a postmaster, an owner of real estate and a developer of land and buildings in town. To say he was a successful businessman is not enough. He was an entrepreneur. His demeanor was serious, down to earth, straight and honest. Never a glad-hander, nor a gregarious handshaker, he was true business.

Frank owned the trading post on the New River. His trade with the Native Americans was productive. The 1900 census listed 52 persons in Fort Lauderdale. For some Floridians, the Seminoles were troublesome folks, who waged three wars with the white Americans and never signed a peace treaty with them. When masses of Seminoles came by boats down the New River with their pelts, produce, animals, handmade creations, they were met at the Stranahan trading post first as customers but eventually as friends. Often they stayed for days, usually sleeping on their front porch.

Ivy Stranahan approached the Seminoles not with tolerance but with an acceptance that meant an equal respect of the two parties involved, a position that opens the worlds between different people, a smile, a touch when agreed to by both people, a way that can lead to love. Teacher Stranahan did not need lesson plans. The curious, dark eyed children sleeping on her porch were her lesson plans. She followed their lead—never disrupting their inquisitiveness about her and her lifestyle. Clothes and sewing must have been early interests especially among the girls. Imagine

Ivy
Stranahan,
FLHS archives

Too Hot To Hide

comparing her needle with theirs. How did they sew their colorful dresses? "Show me," she would say in words or actions. Eventually, that exploration led to her sharing with them the use of her sewing machine that today still sits on display in the Stranahan House. She learned from them, and they learned from her. This gentleness of acceptance led to an exchange and true teaching as Mrs. Ivy began to understand the Seminole ways and they began to understand hers. And with that continuous exchange and understanding of each other came trust.

Both the Stranahans became trustworthy friends of anyone who related to them, especially the Seminoles. As time went on, this trust would prove valuable to the Seminole people and the white American government. While the Stranahans by nature were quiet people, they understood their community and reached out to solve problems. Ivy Stranahan began with the Seminole children who slept on her porch during their parents' time buying and selling at he husband's trading post. She combined her teachings about Christianity (she was raised a Methodist) with offering food such as apples and other fruits unknown to the children. As long as they came to the trading post, her teachings continued.

As a consummate volunteer, a list of her activities throughout her lifetime gives one a sense of her value to the community and shows how she grew as an advocate.

1911   The town's Woman's Civic Improvement Association began with 18 women, including Ivy Stranahan. Later the Association became the Woman's Club of Fort Lauderdale.

1913-1916 Ivy became president of the Women's Club, and to this day she was the only president who served three consecutive terms.

1915   Ivy joined the Seventh Day Adventists Church.

1915   The Florida Federation of Woman's Clubs conservation department exercised control over the Royal Palm State Park which eventually became part of Florida's Everglades Park system. Mrs. Stranahan's task was to monitor this control in South Florida.

1915   She became chair of the Indian Affairs Committee of the Florida Federation of Woman's clubs.

1916-1919 Was President of the Fort Lauderdale Woman's Club.

1917   Ivy joined the Woman's Christian Temperance Union (WCTU).

Stranahan Park, Stranahan High School, Stranahan House.
Author's photos

She convinced her husband not to sell alcohol or any of its derivatives at the trading post.

1917-1918 She became President of the Florida Equal Suffrage Association.

1918 She was appointed chairman of the Broward County Liberty Bond Campaign.

1919 Ivy became secretary of the Woman's Club, and founder of the

1919 Study Club, which was devoted to serious study of events, issues and subjects.

1924 Federal Bureau of Indian Affairs used Mrs. Stranahan's influence to convince the Seminoles to move to new reservation land designated for them.

1925 She became a member of the city's Board of Managers, the first and only woman on that Board at that time.

1926 Thanks in part to Ivy Stranahan's influence, the Seminoles officially secured their reservation land.

1927 Using her positions on the Woman's Club and City Managers Board, she pressed for a home for the aged, the "Haven of Rest."

1930 She testified before the U.S. Senate Indian Affairs Committee. She helped found the group Friends of the Florida Seminoles and served as its Secretary-Treasurer.

1933-34 Ivy advocated for the passage of state legislation of Homestead Exemption Act, which became state law.

1939 She became Treasurer of the Fort Lauderdale Garden Club and the first woman member of the County Welfare Board.

1939 For the price of $10, she sold land to the Board of Education for the "colored" Dillard School for $10.00.

1941 She was Secretary-Treasurer of the Provident Hospital for the "coloreds."

1946 Mrs. Stranahan took part in the formation of the Friends of the Everglades.

1962 She was a member of the founding group of the Fort Lauderdale Historical Society, where she served as trustee.

1963 She established and funded a foundation at the Historical Society.

1971   Ivy Stranahan died at age 90.

When I decided to list Mrs. Stranahan's accomplishments by year, I wanted to show how she grew, in talent and spirit, through the decades and how her involvement mirrored Fort Lauderdale's growth. For example, her beginnings as a teacher of Seminole children led her eventually to join the new non-profit organization Friends of the Seminoles; she became their white spokesperson in Washington D.C. and used herself as a bridge that could be trusted between the Seminoles and the white American government which had a poor reputation for honesty and trust in their historical relations with the Indians. What she did for both the whites and Native Americans was to diminish the friction and fighting between them.

As Mrs. Stranahan became a political activist and advocate for the Seminoles she began to use those same skills in other parts of the community. Her involvement in the formation of the New Provident Hospital, then called the "colored" hospital, showed this growth and development in her. She became a skillful organizer. Using her reputation on one board, she'd network, advocate, gather supporters, shape their support and find funding for the next project. She was the quintessential volunteer. She was aware of her power and learned how to use it to solve community problems. Ivy Stranahan became a community treasure, never to be forgotten in Fort Lauderdale's history. Truly, she was the mother of Fort Lauderdale.

I joined the Woman's Club soon after I came to Fort Lauderdale. I noticed it was close to celebrating its 100th year and with my interest in history, I thought I could add to theirs.

Close to Mrs. Stranahan's heart was the Fort Lauderdale Woman's Club.

Fort Lauderdale Woman's Club (est. 1911)

I suppose one could think of a woman's club as populated by women who knew nothing else to do than to join a club. By definition, these would be women who had no need to work for a salary as they all had husbands who supported them affluently. As some have said, one could poke fun at these oversized ladies who made mountains from molehills and spent much time and energy doing so. However, and there is a large "however" to consider here, I contend such criticisms came from people who essentially had no facts to validate such opinions and did not know what they were talking about. Women's club work, I think, represents the conscience of our culture. As one reads about club work, one cannot help but think: club work so obviously needed to be done, why did no one else think to do it? Maybe because no one else did it, it became very clear that women's clubs needed to do it. Implied is the notion that women see problem solving differently than men do. This is not to say that women or men think better but rather that the two genders really think differently. That difference, when married in action, can result in some extraordinary advances in our culture. This conclusion is apparent as we look at the beginning of the American woman's club movement and the early years of the Woman's Club of Fort Lauderdale.

In America, the first woman's clubs began in the Northeast, New York and Boston to be specific. In New York, Jennie June, the pen name of Jane Cunningham Croly, began the Sorosis Club in April, 1868. On February 16, 1868, Caroline Severence had formed the New England Woman's Club in Boston. Both headed in the direction of relieving women of isolation as homemakers, and supplying knowledge and information they could not get from any other source at a time when formal education was not always available to all women who wanted it. The Sorosis Club mushroomed into the General Federation of Women's Clubs and by 1888, hundreds and thousands of women had joined local woman's clubs.

The clubs formed when women, in some parts of America, were not allowed to speak in public and were reprimanded if they did. Another reason for a woman to join a club was to speak her mind about what troubled her. Committees formed to study issues in house and home, journalism, and philanthropy. During the Civil War women joined the war effort in nursing, supplying food to soldiers, rolling bandages, providing clean clothing and blankets. Keep in mind at that time in the military structure, there was no medical corps. The women in the Sanitary Commission provided such lifesaving services when it became clear that more soldiers died from wounds infected from unsanitary conditions and their diseases than from the actual wounds inflicted by combat. Their work in the Sanitary Commission morphed into what became the Medical Corps of the army.

Self-improvement in its various forms stood high on the list of woman's club's goals. Invariably, certain social actions began to foment. The push, the advocacy of education for women emerged. This need for reform led to the Columbia College in New York City to open its courses to women for the first time in its history. Adult education and evening courses began. Within the structure of the woman's clubs, came the need for organizations to tie together the many clubs in each state. After state structures formed, then a need for the national organization formed to tie together the various state structures. And so the General Federation of Women's Clubs emerged.

Women in Europe and eventually throughout the world began woman's clubs and pressed to achieve certain changes in their local, state and national communities. Mottoes such as "Unity in Action" and "Unity in Diversity" signified a joining of hands as women working together to form a better life for themselves and their families were spurred to change what was wrong to what was right. For many women, if not all, such an avenue of action and achievement was needed in the development of any town's civic structure. Clearly, there was much to be done in forming this new town called Fort Lauderdale. The women dove right into it after they were asked.

On January 11, 1911, the Men's Trade Association asked mostly their wives and some others, 18 women in all, if they would start a women's club. Yes, they would, no question at all about it, and when they did, they founded the Woman's Civic Association even before the town of Fort Lauderdale became officially that in March, 1911.

The next year the new town almost disappeared. A fire raged in the little downtown and even though the flames were yards from a source of water, the New River, no water doused the fire that almost consumed the entire downtown. From that emergency came the realization that a volunteer fire

Tony Tommie and Eva Oliver were both "firsts" in this picture. Tony was the first Seminole child to receive public school education. Eva was the first president of the Fort Lauderdale Woman's Club which with the Daughters of the American Revolution sponsored Tony's first white education.
Fort Lauderdale Historical Society archives

department needed to be formed, post haste, and some equipment to get the water from the New River to the fires needed to be bought. Quick as a wink, the ladies of the Association sent the fire folks a check for $100 possibly to buy the equipment. This sort of quick response one could see all the way though the 100 years of the woman's club involvement with Fort Lauderdale and its needs. However, the ladies were keen on social events to

Transformation of the Woman's Club back to its 1917 original facade. Pictured, left to right: JoAnn Smith, President; Jean Deering, Treasurer; Mae Silver, Corr. Sec.; Gretchen Thompson, Secretary; Valerie Taylor. Back row: Kathy Schauer, Membership chair; Susan McClellan, architect. June, 2011. Author's photo

bring the people of the little town together. To honor the city's first mayor, William H. Marshall, the first ladies association president, Mrs. Eva Bryan Oliver hosted a reception at the Oliver home. It was the big social event of the year.

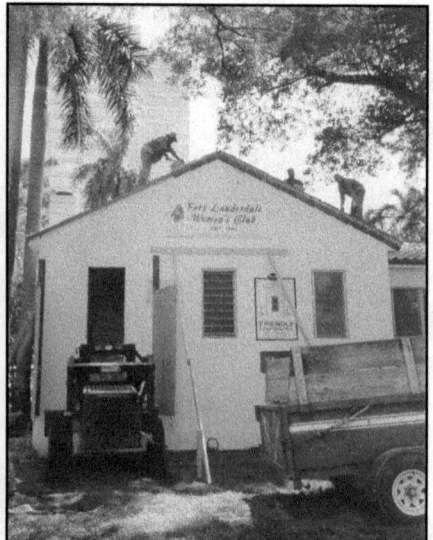

Too Hot To Hide

In 1912 the club affiliated with the Florida Federation of Woman's Clubs and changed its name to the Woman's Club of Fort Lauderdale. It incorporated in 1913 and joined with the General Federation of Women's Clubs in 1914. In addition to creating the structure of the new club with a constitution and by-laws, the women began fundraising for a clubhouse and its site. Until they had their own home, meetings were at churches and club members' homes. Suppers, beach and chowder parties, bazaars and minstrel shows as fund raisers dotted their calendar months.

In tandem with their goal of a clubhouse, the women also wanted a library for there was none in Fort Lauderdale. The ladies envisioned the clubhouse as a beginning library and started massing books from the Florida Federation to fill it.

Following their concern for the education of all children, including Seminoles, with the leadership of president Ivy Stranahan sponsored the first public education of a Seminole child, Tony Tommie. Leaving the state because there were no schools to accept him otherwise, Tony had difficulty at the Indian Industrial School in Carlisle, Pennsylvania. It was too cold for him and he returned home. However, what the women in the club accomplished was an historic breakthrough in the public education of Seminole children. Neither the white establishment nor the Seminoles were supportive of what the club women did at that time. Eventually all the Tommie boys secured a public education and became important leaders in bridging the cultural gap between the whites and the Seminoles and in mending the wounds still raw from the three wars between them.

In reviewing the accomplishments of the first decade of the Woman's Club, one cannot help but be astonished at the outcome. While working to fund their clubhouse and site, the women continued their outreach into

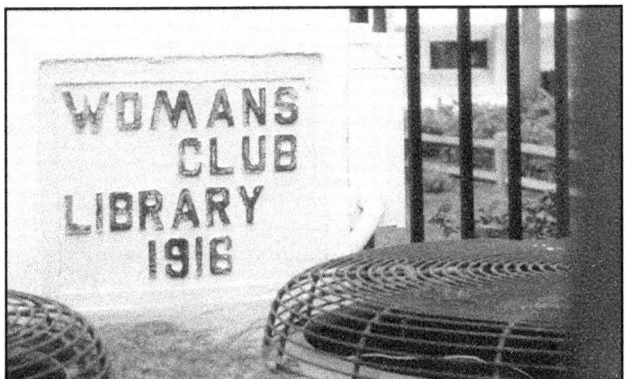

Woman's Club Library plaque on the side of the building notes the beginning of the public library in Fort Lauderdale at this site in 1916.
Author's photo

Fort Lauderdale Woman's Club original 18 members who said "Yes" when the Men's Trade Association asked them to form a club in 1911. First called the Women's Civic Improvement Association it began two months earlier than the city of Fort Lauderdale. This 1922 picture includes, in the first row, left to right: Mrs. John Sherman, Mrs. Luella Snyder (president with gavel), Mrs. Clausen. Second row: Mrs. Eva Oliver (first president), Mrs. Belle Goodrich, Mrs. Frank Stranahan, Mrs. TenBrook, Mrs. Heimberger; Third row: Mrs. Louise Richardson, Mrs. Kermit Richardson, Mrs. Henry Shackelford. Between rows: Mrs. Lottie Kohlhousen, Mrs. Elizabeth Kraft, Mrs. R.D. Bailey. Back row: Mrs. Lucille Quinn, Mrs. S.J. Gilliam, Mrs. W.C. Learid, Mrs. Samuel Clark, Mrs. Fred Shippey.

the community. The Girls Canning Club and the Boys Corn Club both forerunners of the 4-H Club, benefitted from the Woman's Club sponsorship. It fundraised for the city band and presented it with $50. The club bought a Victrola, bought a piano and helped the band with a Fourth of July celebration. The women joined the Trade Association to weed and clean up the local cemetery and continued their push to cleanup yards and streets throughout the town. They raised funds to support the schools with expense and building accounts and entertained public school teachers at a special reception. When the editor of the *Fort Lauderdale Herald* took some time off, the women published the paper so none of the vacationers in town would miss the news.

Ivy Stranahan became president, from 1913 to 1916, and to this day was the only president in the history of the club who held that post for three consecutive terms. Two building lots came into the ownership of the Club. In 1913, Mr. and Mrs. Wheeler and Mr. and Mrs. Stranahan gave properties on which the club could build its clubhouse. The Stranahan gift became the site of the clubhouse we see today. The ladies engaged August Geiger, an architect of note in those days, to design their place. Geiger, a native of New Haven, Connecticut, had a reputation for creating buildings in the Mediterranean style, and the clubhouse was his seventh project. The George Young Construction Company built the clubhouse, which was ready for occupancy on May 18, 1917. The cost was about $4,500 and the mortgage was $2,800.

Mrs. Katherine Wheeler, president, suggested the hibiscus as the club's flower and its colors of red and green. Mrs. Alice Drake penned the club motto:

For the cause that need assistance,

For the wrongs that need resistance,

For the future in the distance

And the good that we may do.

With a new clubhouse and with most of the parts of the club developed, the Fort Lauderdale Woman's Club, like all of America faced World War I in 1917. Its energy was dominated by the war effort. The Florida Federation president, Mrs. Edgar Lewis stated, "We have adjusted and are adjusting every department of work to meet the needs of these shifting times."[5] She spoke for all the state federations and clubs with those words. The Red Cross emerged during this time as an avenue of assistance from and to and by the Woman's Club. It often used the clubhouse for its many programs. The rationing of food and therefore an equal concern about healthful eating during the rationing became an opportunity to teach canning, home vegetable/fruit gardening, and other strategies for the homemaker. In response to this, the club began a program to study foods and their nutritional values provided by Mrs. Peay, the county's demonstration agent.She demonstrated cheese-making, jelly-making and the need for a balanced diet.

The government asked citizens to go without meat one day, without bread one day, without sweets another day. These requests had to be weighed against a finding that occurred during the draft inspections of men for the armed forces. Remarkably, almost one third of the draftees were rejected because of neglect stemming from childhood. Physical defects as a result of parental ignorance about nutrition resulted in our army losing an important force needed during wartime.[6] Therefore, while rationing was needed what also was needed was instruction to parents about good eating, good foods and their value to the health of a child. The club did its job in attending to this need.

The club burst into contributions to many charities: War Children's Relief Fund, Children's Home Society of Florida and Jacksonville, European Relief Council, Near East Relief Fund, Florida Industrial School, and Serbian Child Welfare Fund. On Memorial Day, members planted trees to honor their fallen dead soldiers. On Washington's birthday, 100 coconut and Australian pine trees decorated the town.

The 18 charter members of the club were: Mrs. H. B. Adams, Mrs. S.M. Davis, Mrs. G.I. Edgerton, Mrs. J.K. Gordon Mrs. W.H. Heiney, Mrs. W. H. Marshall, Mrs. P.D. Parks, Mrs. C. G. Rhodes, Mrs. D.D. Rawlins, Mrs. C.H. Slifer, Mrs. Frank Stranahan, Mrs. W. Snyder, Mrs. D.G. TenBrook, Mrs. Chas. Van Antwerp, Mrs. J.B. Vreeland, Mrs. H.G. Wheeler and Mrs. Frank R. Oliver.

Presidents during this first decade were: Mrs. Frank R. Oliver, Mrs. DeWitt, Mrs. Greenfield Ten Brook, Mrs. Katherine Wheeler Hyat, Mrs. Frank Stranahan, Mrs. Belle Goodrich, Mrs. B. L. Smith, Mrs. Edward Heimberger and Mrs. George E. Henry.

The second decade of the Woman's Club heralded new challenges and programs. Some, like the public library, had begun the decade before and now with 1200 books filling the clubhouse, it was time for the city to create a public library. A library board of directors emerged in 1925. The club continued to fund and support the library in many ways. The club's funding of the public library reflected the history of woman's clubs throughout America. The American Library Association stated that Woman's Clubs had founded 85 percent of the public libraries in the United States.[7]

As the women's concerns centered on public education for Seminole children, they also advocated an nine-month school year for black children. Previously, these children had only a seventh-month school year and spent two months picking vegetables in the fields. These women of the Woman's Club stepped outside the mainstream thinking when they advocated education for Seminole and colored children. Their advocacy for children's education, regardless of skin color, showed boldness and bravery. Clearly, their leadership opened paths of liberation for both the Seminoles and the African-Americans which they pursued in later years.

Continuing their concern for children, a club committee became active in court cases that involved young girls. This committee eventually formed the Broward Welfare Board which until it became part of city government, furnished volunteers to do the social work. In 1926 the committee suggested to the County Commissioners that a paid worker needed to be hired.

In 1925, the Club began a program that exists even to its 100th year. The Educational Loan Fund began as a loan available to young women who wanted to attend college. After college, the students returned the loan so that it could be used for others. Through the years, the Loan Fund became an outright scholarship to worthy applicants. Currently, the Broward Community College manages the scholarship which the Woman's Club funds each year. If one assumes that two students each year received a loan/scholarship, then 150 young women can attribute help for their college education to the Woman's Club.

The women were entrepreneurial. They bought two lots in Riveria for speculation and received as a gift three lots in Croissant Park for a clubhouse site. The YMCA became the recipient of these three lots when the clubhouse used the Stranahan donation instead.

When one stands before the clubhouse today, one can proudly say, it survived all the hurricanes, even the devastating one of 1926. The clubhouse suffered only a broken window and other minor damages when most of downtown Fort Lauderdale collapsed. Women wrote about installation of officers meeting amidst mattresses for refugees that still covered the floor. Homeless men found the clubhouse a comfortable place to stay until they got themselves a new place. Since the hurricane damaged so much of the town's landscape, the women raised funds to plant trees and shrubs on Las Olas Blvd. from Andrews Ave. to the beach.

The Port Authority needed help to rename the Port and came to the Woman's Club with that request. The club's first president, Mrs. Eva Oliver, formed a committee and after much investigation, wrote a resolution that renamed the Lake Mabel Harbor into Port Everglades. The well-written resolution showed the vision of these women that this Port would one day become extremely important in the future growth of Fort Lauderdale. They were right. They requested the surrounding Woman's Clubs to support this name. On January 13, 1928 Port Everglades became a new name on the map of Fort Lauderdale.

Dania's "Haven for Rest" home for the aged became a project on which the club assisted the County Commissioners with.

Presidents during this second decade were: Mrs. George Henry, Mrs. Ellie Newton Sperry, Mrs. Louella C. Giles Snyder, Mrs. Nina Y. Bailey, Mrs. Alfred John Beck, Mrs. M. Lewis Hall, Mrs. J. B. Vreeland, Sr., Mrs. Robert E. Dye.

The third decade of the Club saw such an increase in membership that new chairs were bought to allow members to "sit soft." They also bought a second piano.

Outreach consisted of purchasing a rug for the Haven for Rest; sponsoring the City Band, which gave concerts in the park and also assisted schools with music; sponsoring the first Girl Scout troop and funding the leader's uniform; purchasing layette for the Salvation Army; furnishing a room at Broward Hospital; dressing dolls for the Salvation Army; and forming a committee to continue funding the Library, repair books and buy new books.

Presidents during the third decade were: Mrs. George A. Carlisle, Mrs. Meade Neel, Mrs. Clarence Adams, Mrs. Louis G. Richardson, Mrs. Frank S. Dodd, Mrs. Harlow G. Holabird, Mrs. Logan Taylor Brown and Mrs. Benjamin D. Arnold.

World War II dominated and focused specific projects during the fourth decade of the Club. To encourage the sale of war bonds, the General National began a special "Buy a Bomber" competition among the State Federations. The cost quoted for a heavy bomber was $300,000, $175,000 for a medium bomber, and $75,000 for a fighter pursuit plane. A plane would be named for a group of clubs, a state or an individual town. The total bonds sold by the General Federation of State Clubs was a staggering $101,617,750. Many bombers carried the names of Woman's Clubs on them, including Fort Lauderdale Woman's Club which bought enough bonds to buy a fighter plane. The Club staffed the Service Men's Club with entertainment and food one day a week.

Even though building materials, as most other materials, were scarce to find, the club engaged in an expansion of the clubhouse and changed the front of the building from Andrews Ave. to S.E. First Street in 1949. The remodeling even included a new kitchen. The cost was $22,650. The club began its first antique show to raise funds for the rebuilding.

Notable to mention is that during this decade a number of women, for the first time in our nation's history, began to run for public office. Mrs. George W. Young, also known to the club as Virginia Young, ran for mayor and succeeded in winning two nonconsecutive terms as mayor of Fort Lauderdale. She remains to this day as the first and only woman mayor of Fort Lauderdale.

Presidents during the fourth decade were: Mrs. Ernest Bratzel, Mrs. Joseph H. Brown, Mrs. John C. Grimm, Mrs. George W. Young, Mrs. F. M. Knight, Mrs. Harold A. Wayne and Mrs. H. W. Ecker.

In this brief summary of the work of the early years of the Woman's Club in Fort Lauderdale, one can see how the club exerted leadership in many areas of community life. The Woman's Club managed to build its own Clubhouse and its own organization while simultaneously shaping some departments of the civic government of Fort Lauderdale, contributing to the town's charities, and responding to the national calls that came from world wars. One admires how flexible and visionary the women were in many areas.

Several times, as in the case of education of Seminole and African-American children, one sees the Woman's Club leading the community regarding the importance of education of all citizens, regardless of color, to make our community better. Again, starting the public library showed how women understood that education in a democracy is fundamental to the growth of the town and America. That education, they reasoned, had to be available to all, not just a select few.

Women's history shows us how often women are called upon "to clean things up" and so one can see how often the Woman's Club cleaned things up: getting downtown furnished with garbage bins, getting legislation passed to prohibit farm animals from downtown, privies in the school years, etc. etc.

While so many of us growing up might get bothered by our mothers, aunts, etc. who pushed us to keep our hands clean, we know, as scientists have now proved, how basic such a procedure is in maintaining good health.

One sees examples of the clubwomen who started a program, like their involvement regarding girls and the court, worked it for a few years, then turned it into the Welfare Department with paid staff. The library is another example of how the club began a program that turned into the structure of city government.

What this recitation does not say is how the women did it.

Without exception, they all had families. How did they balance home and club life? An observer might state, "Well, they did not have to work for a living." That was true, to some extent. We shall never know about all the women who lost their husbands, like Ivy Stranahan who struggled to pay all the unpaid bills, kept themselves going and continued the club work. Their life stories still remain locked away in the memories of their family members. However, and nevertheless, their voices resonate clearly as we marvel at the work they did for Fort Lauderdale. Often people think that Ivy Stranahan was the first president of the Fort Lauderdale Woman's Club, but that was not so. It was Eva Oliver.

Eva Ann Bryan Oliver (1883-1964)

One sees in Eva Oliver, a pioneer woman of many firsts in Fort Lauderdale but also a woman who wrote about her life and the life of Fort Lauderdale. Behind these first accomplishments was a woman who was brave, generous, talented and intelligent in how she lived her life in Fort Lauderdale.

Since one of her main talents was that of a writer, here are Mrs. Oliver's own words about her arrival in Fort Lauderdale in 1900. Her 6/14/53 article was in the *Miami Herald* (see page 45).

As one can read, at the age of 17, Eva Bryan did not aim to go to college but instead went to work picking tomatoes to help her family. And pick she did, so much so that in some of her other writings she said she picked tomatoes so hard that she never wanted to see another one, not even in a salad, for the rest of her life. Such was the emotional impact of those early hard years on her. But hard work or maybe anything hard about life did not make her a morose or withdrawn person. On the contrary, she opened herself generously to help others in Fort Lauderdale all through her life.

She arrived in Fort Lauderdale as women had arrived in San Francisco during the Gold Rush days, to find a lot of men and very few women.

Bachelors were very lonely for good food and companionship. Within two years, Eva Bryan married Frank Oliver. She was the first white American woman to be married in Fort Lauderdale, and she ended up with a man who was so shy that his participation in social events was limited to peeking through the windows at the dancing inside. However, once he took some dancing lessons, he gained the confidence to enthusiastically join the crowd in the dancing hall.

With the arrival of the railroad in 1896, commerce and business had also arrived.

There were jobs for the men. Frank availed himself of opportunities to open a business. He became president of the National Bank. Soon the Olivers had five healthy children all of whom lived to adulthood.

After the men of the Trade Association invited the ladies of the town to their 1911 meeting at the Southside Methodist Church and asked them to form a club, guess who became the first president of the Ladies

Newspaper picture of Mrs. Oliver ca. 1906, with infant son Louis, and daughter Margaret.

1895 Freeze Ruined Citrus, Sent Her to Fort Lauderdale

Editor The Herald: You might say that I came to Fort Lauderdale from necessity.

When the big freeze of 1895 killed most of the orange groves in middle Florida, the men of families were forced to seek some kind of work to support their families.

My father, Louis H. Bryan, came to Fort Lauderdale in 1895 to help build the 10 miles of railroad south of New river. When he returned home with stories of the wonderful country, all of the family wanted to move here but the people of Florida were very poor after the freeze.

As soon as I was old enough, I decided to try and earn some money for the move. I came in 1900 to visit a sister and pack tomatoes. After two years of very hard work, my family came. There were only a few real houses. Most everyone lived in palmetto houses at first, some with dirt floors.

The tomato industry was new at that time, prices for winter vegetables were good and everyone soon had a home. After two years I married one of the town's bachelors and we had a family of five children.

As I look back I give all the credit to God for directing us to Broward county and am just happy to have had a part in doing what we could.

EVA A. OLIVER,
1000 SE Eighth st.,
Fort Lauderdale

Our Town Pioneer

Presented to _Mrs. Frank R. Oliver_

in recognition of your faith in the land and your foresightedness and devotion to

Fort Lauderdale---Our Town

Your example and civic pride is an inspiration for generations to come

Coral Ridge Inc.

James S. Hunt. - President

Stephen A. Calder. - Secretary

January 22, 1954

Our Town Pioneer certificate honoring Eva Oliver, 1954.

Improvement Society? Eva Oliver, of course. Later that Society became called the Fort Lauderdale Woman's Club (whom we met in the previous chapter). One of the first big social events in town was a reception organized by the Woman's Club for the town's first mayor, William Marshall. The Olivers opened their beautiful house on the New River for this party. The lawn setting along the river provided a stunning background for the ladies in their large feathered hats, long training skirts and petticoats, and high buttoned shoes. It was a time to remember and the talk of the town.

But those days were different from the early times Mrs. Oliver recalled.

> *"The first homes of these pioneers were very poor and inconvenient. I have seen and lived in every kind. First, usually a tent with a dirt floor next a palmetto shack still with a dirt floor. As soon as possible a real floor was added and to add to the discomfort you could hear snakes crawling round in the palmetto. As far as I can remember, my father was the only person to build a palmetto house with rooms, a floor and porch. From this house I was married."*

Mrs. Oliver was the only mother whose five children joined the military in WWII. Front row: Staff Sgt. Margaret Oliver Crews, WAC and her mother Eva Oliver. Back row: Chief Boatswain's mate Joe B. Oliver, USNR Private Frank R. Oliver Jr. (killed in action), Specialist First Class James C. Oliver, USNR, and Electrician's mate Louis B Oliver, USNR.   Fort Lauderdale Historical Society archives

In an article about her life, titled "Don't Retire from Active Life", she remembered her early years:

> *"I wish I could picture for you my first home. All my life I had hoped to have a home of my own. I will try to describe it. It was 12x14 in size, one room, made with building paper canvas, a little lumber very economical as you could sit on the edge of the bed and eat your meals.*
>
> *"I was very proud of this home."*[8]

The Olivers eventually had a big beautiful home. And during the Depression, Mrs.Oliver ran a tea shop in her home called the River View Inn. Here she helped people get jobs and certainly made sure they had food to eat. Her son, James Oliver said of her in 1953, "She takes care of more people than a professional organization, is on the go from morning till night just helping people..."[9]

Mrs. Oliver's talent as a writer gave her the opportunity to become the town's first historian. Her history of Fort Lauderdale appeared in a series of articles in *The Free Press* from 1936 to 1937. She was the first to compile and write the history of the town she loved from her personal recollections. The Fort Lauderdale Historical Society received these documents for use by further historians.

To make this piece complete, these activities in her life must be mentioned. She was the mother of the first white American girl born in Fort Lauderdale, the first woman to drive a car in Fort Lauderdale (although she thought she might have been the first in South Florida) one of the first members of the Fort Lauderdale Garden Club, Eastern Star and Fort Lauderdale Historical Society, and the first baptized in the New River with the First Baptist Church, and the first woman on the local election board after women won the right to vote. When the town's commissioners approached the Woman's Club to rename Port Mabel, Mrs. Oliver served as the chairman of the three women committee and renamed Port Mabel, Port Everglades.

In 1954 Fort Lauderdale recognized Mrs. Oliver with a certificate "In recognition of your faith in the land your foresightedness and devotion to Fort Lauderdale—Our Town." In 1961 the town recognized Mrs. Oliver on the occasion of its golden anniversary as a person who was in residence when the city was incorporated. In 1992 Broward County's first Women's Hall of Fame nominated her for her significant contribution to society and to the progress and freedom of women.

During World War II, Mrs. Oliver was perhaps the only mother in Fort Lauderdale whose five children, four sons and one daughter, were all members of the armed forces. Frank Oliver Jr. died in the War and in his honor the Disabled American Veteran's Auxiliary Unit 40 was named. Mrs. Oliver actively participated in the Veteran's Auxiliary as a Gold Star Mother.

A good friend to Ivy Stranahan and one who served as president of the Woman's Club, was Annie Beck. Like Ivy, she had no children and therefore could give her time to the world of flowers in Fort Lauderdale. Often she and Ivy served on charity boards together. Annie's devotion and expertise to plants put her in the founding group of the Fort Lauderdale Garden Club.

Annie Beck (1886-1985)

Leaving a considerable legacy of volunteerism and community organizing on behalf of plants, flowers and environmental issues, Annie Beck lived to ninety-nine years of age. She arrived with her husband Alfred Beck, the town's pharmacist, in Fort Lauderdale on December 1, 1916. Very soon after moving here, Mrs. Beck founded the women's auxiliary of the Episcopal Church. From a botanical point of view, she had definite ideas that would improve the town. She created organizations such as the Fort Lauderdale Garden Club which today remains a vigorous organization involved in the plant life of the community. As a close friend of Ivy Stranahan, she often was part of the organizations that Ivy joined or formed. Both women saw how they could better the town, and so Annie also served as the president of the Fort Lauderdale Woman's Club. The Mango Forum and the Advisory Park Board benefitted from her membership. As she immersed herself in the plant life of Fort Lauderdale she amassed an outstanding collection of botanical and horticultural books that now resides in the clubhouse in Birch Park. The disaster of the 1926 hurricane changed Annie Beck's life. Even though the great storm created winds so powerful that they destroyed the roof of her house, she observed that native plants weathered the severity of the storm better than the exotics. Then she decided, or rather, insisted, that native plants and tropical

Two photos of Annie Beck's house; the old one (1913) and the newly restored one in Middle River Terrace Park.
Photos by author

plants should be planted in town. Furthermore, as another offspring of the hurricane and at the urging of Annie Beck, the Fort Lauderdale Garden Club emerged in 1927.

When I called the Garden Club to arrange for a time to visit and photograph Annie Beck's library collection, I spoke to Ann Schandelmayer, a club member and a friend of Annie Beck's. (see Sources). Ann told me she had been busy watching the house being moved. " What house?" I asked.

"Why, Annie Beck's house. It had just been moved to Middle River Terrace Park, yesterday, July 17, 2008. The plan is for the house to be renovated and used as a community center." Since Annie Beck's organization work was not only local but statewide, the house could serve the various communities well.

Talking to Ann Schandelmayer about Annie, I wondered to her if Annie had a photographic memory which could serve her well as a botanist. She did not think so but knew that Annie Beck simply knew all the plants

Too Hot To Hide

On the way to a new home

Newspaper picture of Annie Beck's house being moved to its new site, July 28, 2008. Sun-Sentinel

by botanical as well as casual names. Called on often to conduct plant walks, she had little difficulty speaking about everything she saw. When I asked about her personality, Ann gave this example. During her tenure as president of the Garden Club, she was in the position to clean up some roadways in town. She had access to a truck, the driver and his assistant. At her direction one day they cleared five truckloads of commercial signs from roadways and sent them elsewhere. The driver and his assistant expressed concern about the scope of this cleanup. Would they get in trouble? They were nervous. Annie's response was, "If you go to jail, then I'll go with you." The two decided if this 80-year-old lady would go to jail with them, they'd go along with the cleanup. Some merchants expressed unhappiness about their disappeared signs, but that was all there was to it. She recommended plants in place of placards.

On her 90th birthday, December 4, 1976, almost 60 years to the day of her arrival in Fort Lauderdale, the city named her Citizen of the Year and named a park after her. The Annie Beck Park located on the Victoria Park Boulevard contains the magnificent flowering *Tabebuia Argenta* trees, Annie's favorite, that burst into resplendent lush yellow blossoms each spring. This was Annie's signature tree and she called it "the Las Olas Tree."

Another Annie who was indispensable to Ivy Stranahan was Annie Reed, her housekeeper and cook. When I learned that Annie Reed somehow

Tababuia Argenta fronts the Annie Beck Park in Victoria Park (top). The Argenta in bloom (left).

Photos by author

figured into the story of how the African-Americans received the land for their second school (eventually called Dillard School) through the Stranahans—I wanted to discover that story. The details remained clouded in history. To unravel the mystery, I went to the African-American Library and Museum. No information was there. However, I was put in touch with Mrs. Walters who lived with Mrs. Reed for many years. Mrs. Reed was a leader in her community particularly in the Mt. Hermon Church. I learned from Mrs. Ellyn Walters that Annie Reed's Board was to celebrate its 100th anniversary in a few days. Of course I attended.

Too Hot To Hide

Annie Thomas Reed (1883-1955)

Somewhere in the pages of early history there must be an old adage that says when two good women get together something special is bound to happen. I heard the story that Annie Reed had something to do with getting the land for the new colored school. The person who came forth with the land was Frank Stranahan. Since there are no records to explain this happening, I was curious how the information about the need for a new colored school became known to Mrs. Stranahan. When I spoke to Mrs. Walters, who lived with Mrs. Reed for many years, and asked her about this, she thought that when Ivy Stranahan drove her housekeeper Annie Reed home at the end of each work day, likely their conversation included a discussion about the needed land.

Once they decided about that need, it seemed reasonable for Ivy to put the idea to her husband who owned a lot of land in town. As the Board of Education minutes of July 3, 1923 read: "A resolution approving purchase of real estate from Frank Stranahan, as a school site, by the trustees of special tax school district number three of Broward County, Florida."[10] The sum stated was $4500. Harry Weidling sold to the Board of Education an adjoining lot for $1.00. While it seemed that was the transaction that transferred ownership of the land from Stranahan to the Board of Education for the new colored school, I was not sure and investigated further the chapter titled "The Missing Deed". Read on.

Photo of Annie Reed from
My Soul is Witness, *p. 31.*
Mrs. Walters collection

We know much about Ivy Stranahan but little of Annie Reed. Annie Thomas of St. Augustine married T.B. Reed of Tallahassee on June 9, 1910. Mr. Reed worked for Mr. Stranahan for a while but it was Mrs. Reed who became an important member of the Stranahan household for many years. According to Mrs. Walters whom I interviewed, the two women probably had an unusually close relationship since neither had children but had a great concern for the welfare of all children. Mrs. Walters became almost an adopted child to Mrs. Reed as she boarded with her while attending Dillard School for many years in Fort Lauderdale. In fact, when Ellyn Ferguson became

Mrs. Walters, she married from Mrs. Reed's house. It was from Mrs. Walters that I learned about a centennial celebration of Annie Reed's Board to be held at Mt. Hermon A.M.E. Church on August 23, 2009.

At this event, I learned about Annie Reed's church Board. Mrs. Reed was president for the

Annie Reed's Board at the Mt. Hermon Church. Author took this picture on occasion of the 100th anniversary of Annie's Board, Sept. 9, 2009. First row, left to right: Eddye LaBell, Nellie Jackson, Augustine McDaniel, Clara Higden. Second row: Judy Johnson, Maple Merritt, Suzye Johnson, Mildred Jones-Fuce. Mrs. Nellie Jackson is president.

women's Board's first 47 years. This auxiliary board essentially served to fundraise for the church and eventually for the school. Remarkably, after her only four more women were president. The women's group raised funds in many of the usual ways: bake sales, cruises, auctions, raffles, fashion shows etc. Mrs. Reed also served as a class leader whose task it was to look after certain members of the church. In those early times when intolerance and prejudice prevailed, her advice and direction helped church members

Annie's Board members, in their anniversary outfits, in front of Mt. Hermon Church.

Author's photo

Too Hot To Hide

find their way using common sense and love. Annie Reed's Board is still very active and their focus helped create the new K-12 charter school across the street. When I asked Mrs. Nellie Jackson, the current president of Annie's Board, how much money the Board had raised all these 100 years, she reckoned it was about $120,000. "And tell me about only five presidents in 100 years," I asked. Mrs. Jackson replied in effect that once you are president, you are there for life or as long as the Lord keeps you healthy enough to serve.

Dillard School, the second "colored" school, now a National Historic Landmark, library and cultural, museum center.   Author's photo

Mrs. Walters described Annie Reed, also known as Mother Reed, as a woman quiet but well spoken and well read. As a member of Eastern Star, Mrs. Reed extended herself into the community at large, that place across the railroad tracks. Although Mrs. Reed was a person only five feet in height, she used every inch of it on behalf of her community. Annie Thomas Reed's dedication and devotion to her church and her community made Fort Lauderdale what it is today. Her memory serves to inspire us all to carry on in her tradition of service and love.

I had a "thing" about wanting to find the deed that transferred ownership from Frank Stranahan to the Board of Education in 1923 or thereabouts. So I was determined to track down some record of the action that transferred Stranahan land to the Board of Education. I'm going to spin this journey to uncover the mystery for you. Stay with me.

The Missing Deed

Where was the deed that verified Frank Stranahan's sale to the Board of Education of the land on which the colored school was built in 1924? I'm going to take you on this journey as it turned out for me. Sometimes it's fun to see how and where I go to find the answer to an historical mystery.

The story in Fort Lauderdale's history is that in 1924 Frank Stranahan sold that property for $1.00 to the Board of Education for the colored school, called the Dillard School, now used as a museum and library, and designated on the National Register. The possible transaction I stated earlier looked promising and fit the story often repeated in town. But I wanted to see the deed or the financial transaction that changed the property from Stranahan to the Board of Education. First I went to the Stranahan collection of invoices, bills etc. at the Hoch Center, Fort Lauderdale Historical Society. No statement of the deed or the transaction that created a deed to the Board of Education was found. Next, I went to the Dillard School Museum. I thought maybe they had a copy of the deed to the property the School sat on. No. I asked if they knew about Annie Reed, the Stranahan's housekeeper who was pivotal in suggesting to Mrs. Stranahan that the colored children needed a new school and a new site to build on. No, Mr. James Bradley, the oral historian there, knew little about her.

Then I thought to look further into Annie Reed and for that I went to the African-American Library and Museum. Not much beyond the book *My Soul is a Witness* showed up about Annie Reed. But, the Special Collections Librarian, Kala Luzia, knew of someone who knew Annie Reed, and she gave me her name and number. When I called her and explained that I wanted to learn about Annie Reed, she took my name and number to pass on to Mrs. Ellyn Walters. The next day Mrs. Walters called me and although I was all right about talking to her over the phone, she graciously invited me to her house for the interview. I learned little specifics about the deed but much about Mrs. Reed, which appears in the previous chapter. Coincidentally, I also learned about the centennial of Annie Reed's Board at the Mt. Hermon Church which I described above.

At the Mt. Hermon Church I met the current members of Annie Reed's

July 3, 1923.

To the Board of Public Instruction,
Broward County, Florida.

Gentlemen:
            We wish to advise that we as Trustees for Special
Tax School District Number Three of Broward County, Florida,
have purchased the following real estate as school sites,
upon the terms and conditions herein named, and desire your
approval of our action in creating these obligations.

            The North Half of Lot 19, being approximately 300
feet deep, of Block 14 of the Town of Fort Lauderdale, Florida,
according to map or plat thereof as made by C.E.Knowlton, C.E.

This land is purchased from Mr. Frank Stranahan, on contract
for the sum of $4500.00 Dollars, to be due and payable May 1st,
1925, with interest from date at six per cent per annum, payable semi-annually. We assume all Taxes levied or assessed for
the year 1923.

                        Respectfully,
                        R. G. Snow,
                        R.E.Dye, TRUSTEES.

            Thereupon J.P.Smoak indtoduced the following resolution
which was approved by both members of the Board.

            A RESOLUTION APPROVING PURCHASE OF
            REAL ESTATE FROM FRANK STRANAHAN, AS A
            SCHOOL SITE, BY THE TRUSTEES OF SPECIAL
            TAX SCHOOL DISTRICT NUMBER THREE OF BRO-
            WARD COUNTY, FLORIDA.

            WHEREAS, The Trustees of Special Tax School District
Number Three of Broward County, Florida, have reported for approval the purhhase of certain real estate from Frank Stranahan, as a
school site in special tax school district number three, and ;

            WHEREAS, The Board of Public Instruction of Broward
County, in regular sessions have considered said purchase, and
the terms thereof, and believe that said purchase is fair and
reasonable, and that the necessity therefor exists.

            Therefore, Be It Resolved, by the Board of Public
Instruction of Broward County, Florida, that the purchase of the
North half of lot 19, being approximately 300 feet deep, of Block
14 of the town of Fort Lauderdale, Florida, according to map or
plat thereof as made by C.E.Knowlton, C.E. from Frank Stranahan,
for the sum of $4500.00, payable May 1st, 1925, with interest from
date at six per cent per annum, payable semi-annually, all taxes
for the year 1923 being assumed by the district, be, and the same
is hereby approved.

                        F. L. Mizell
                        CHAIRMAN

ATTEST.

_____
            Secretary.

            The following option for the purchase of one lot from
Harry Weidling in the Lyons Addition of Fort Lauderdale was presented by the Trustees and its approval recommended by them.

            "For and In Consideration of One Dollar paid to Harry Weidl-
ing by Broward County School Trustee, the said Harry Weidling

*The minutes of the Board of Education dated July 3, 1923 showed what could
be Frank Stranahan's sale of his property to the Board for the Dillard School.
However, research proved that property was not the site of the Dillard School.*

Board that she presided over for 47 years. Mrs. Jackson, the president, arranged for the ladies of the current Annie's Board and I to meet so I could take the picture of them that appears on page 54.

Still wanting to find the deed, I went to the Broward County Board of Education. Jonathan Peservich, director of the real estate department, gave me a copy of the deed dated 1939 when Ivy Stranahan sold the Dillard School property to the Board of Education for $10. There was no other deed there, no other documentation about the sale of the property in 1923. Delores Burrell then led me to the room that housed the Board of Education historical minutes. Reading through 1923 and 1924, I found a citation on July 3, 1923 that showed Frank Stranahan's sale of property for $4500 to the Board of Education. There was no comment about what the property would be used for. But the date was right because the Dillard School was built in 1924. With Renata Turcios' help I secured a copy of those minutes containing the block and lot number of the land.

But, could I be sure that was the land the Dillard School was built on?

Next, I went to the government building to do a title search. Reading microfilm of deeds 1923 to 1924, I found no deed citing the transaction I'd discovered in the Board minutes. I did find the deed recorded for the 1938 transfer. Why was there no recorded deed for Frank Stranahan's sale to the Board of Education in 1923?

I returned to the Hoch Center which has a collection of Sanborn map books and earlier plat books. I wished to verify if the lot and block numbers in the July 3, 1923 minutes belonged to the Dillard property. Those books would tell me. When I presented Chris Barfield, Collections Curator, with the mystery, he found the plat books to unravel the mystery of the July 3, 1923 property. To our dismay, that property was not that of Dillard but of another school in another part of town. However, while the old maps were open, we clarified that the 1939 deed of the sale of the property by Ivy Stranahan to the School Board was, yes, it was the property of the Dillard School.

It seemed I had to accept the fact that there was no deed showing Frank Stranahan's sale of the Dillard School property to the Board of Education. The story of his sale of that property for $1.00 was also not true. But I

Too Hot To Hide

182263

WARRANTY DEED

THIS INDENTURE, Made this 17th day of February, A.D. 1938, between Ivy J. Stranahan, as widow and sole heir at law of the estate of Frank Stranahan, deceased, of the County of Broward, in the State of Florida, party of the first part, and the Board of Public Instruction of the County of Broward, in the State of Florida, a body corporate, party of the second part,

WITNESSETH, That the said party of the first part, for and in consideration of the sum of Ten ($10.00) Dollars, and other good and valuable considerations, to her in hand paid by the said party of the second part, the receipt whereof is hereby acknowledged, as granted, bargained and sold to the said party of the second part, and their successors and assigns forever, the following described land, to-wit:

> All of Block 8 of Tuskegee Park, a subdivision of the NE¼ of the SE¼ of Section 4, Township 50, South, Range 42 East, according to the plat thereof recorded in Plat Book 3, page 9, in the office of the Clerk of the Circuit Court of Broward County, Florida, excepting only that portion thereof described in Deed Book 35, page 312, as follows: Commencing at the SE corner of said Block 8, thence North along the East boundary of said Block 200 feet; thence west 220 feet; thence south 200 feet, to the south line of said block; thence east, along the south boundary of said block, to the point of beginning.

And the said party of the first part does hereby fully warrant the title to said land, and will defend the same against the lawful claims of all persons whomsoever.

IN WITNESS WHEREOF, The said party of the first part has hereunto set her hand and seal the day and year first above written.

Signed, sealed and delivered in the presence of us:

Mary f Bassett

Florence Byrd

Ivy J Stranahan (SEAL)

DEED **308** PAGE **17**

STATE OF FLORIDA :

COUNTY OF BROWARD :

   I HEREBY CERTIFY That on this day personally appeared before me, an officer duly authorized to administer oaths and take acknowledgments, Ivy J. Stranahan, a widow, the sole heir at law of the estate of Frank Stranahan, deceased, to me well known and known to me to be the individual described in and who executed the foregoing deed, and acknowledged before me that she executed the same freely and voluntarily for the purposes therein expressed.

   WITNESS my hand and official seal at Fort Lauderdale County of Broward and State of Florida, this ___17th___ day of February, A.D. 1938.

Florence Byrd
Notary Public, State of Florida
at large.

My Commission Expires:

April 25, 1939

STATE OF FLORIDA
COUNTY OF BROWARD
This instrument filed for record *1st* day
of *March* 1938 and recorded in book *308*
on page *16*. RECORD VERIFIED.
E. R. BENNETT, Clerk of the Circuit Court
By *Ola May Grant* D. C

However, the warranty deed and Ivy Stranahan's letter to the Board dated April 25, 1939 validated that Ivy sold the site of the Dillard School for $10.
Board of Education files

preferred to hear that from the people who know about real estate in Fort Lauderdale. I returned to the County Records Department and put this question to them. How could a school be built on the piece of property for which here was no recorded deed? Derline Lixe, Document Service Worker, hypothesized that in the old days, transactions were sometimes casual, confirmed with a handshake and not recorded. But just to be sure, she sent me up to the Documents Department where old records existed. "Ask them up there," she said. I did.

Both David C. Crankshaw, Supervisor, and Andre Morrell, Administrative Coordinator, met my mysterious question: how could a school be built on the piece of land the deed of which was not recorded? Their conclusion was like Derline's. The action of the sale was casual, perhaps by a handshake. Then all three of us wrestled with the other question: why did Ivy Stranahan finally record this transaction in 1939? After much back and forth discussion, we came upon this possibility. We decided that Ivy Stranahan decided to "spring clean." Possibly, as she put all of her affairs in order, she came upon this transaction that had never been recorded. To finish it right, she worded the deed properly and sent it to the Board of Education. But she sold the property for $10 and not $1.00! Case closed.

Another Annie was a good friend to Ivy Stranahan. She was Annie Tommie, and her bronze plaque in the historical walkway in Stranahan Park is right above Ivy's. Was that an accident? A coincidence? I like to think it was not. Really, I believe it was a statement about the closeness of their relationship during the tense days of the Seminoles and the whites. Their friendship paved the way for the eventual success of the Seminole story today.

Annie Jumper Tommie (1856-1946)

In 1986 when the Fort Lauderdale Historical Society conceived of an historical sidewalk using bronze plaques set in Stranahan Park, it held a contest asking the public for themes of these plaques. Annie Tommie's name emerged as one of the winners. When I saw it, I realized I had little knowledge of this formidable woman. The narrative on her plaque reads:

"Born in the Everglades during the third Seminole war, Annie Tommie grew up in an era during which the Seminoles lived in isolation, making infrequent contacts with the small population of settlers in southern Florida. Her father, Johnny Jumper, farmed land on the north side of the New River near Tarpon Bend. By the turn of the century, Annie had achieved a position of authority within the tribe. She served as a Medicine woman to Seminoles who lived locally as well as those residing deep in the Everglades. One of her sons, Tony Tommie, was the first Seminole to attend local public school.

"Urban development of Florida's lower eastern coast and drainage of the Everglades had, by 1926, disrupted the traditional live styles of many Seminoles. When the federal government established a reservation west of Dania, Annie Tommie led her family there to resettle.

Annie Tommie remained an influential figure within the Seminole tribe and was viewed as a matriarch by the non-Indian population."

Behind these words, was a very important woman. Why? I wondered. Whether by chance or plan, her plaque is followed by Ivy Stranahan's. These two women, Ivy from the white American world, and Annie from the Native-American Seminole world, knew each other. Even more so, if they had not been friends, the history of the reservation land that now houses the Seminole Hard Rock Cafe and Casino enterprise, might have been very different.

The tug of war between the white men in charge of caring for the Seminoles carried on for years. It seemed that none of these white men consulted with or asked the Seminoles what they wanted for their life under the protection of the government—or if they wanted "protection" at

Annie Tommie, medicine woman of her tribe.
Fort Lauderdale Historical Society

all. White men presumed they knew what was best for their Indian charges whom most regarded as little more than children who needed white men's direction. The government built schools, and employed teachers for the Seminoles who refused to send their children to learn the white man's ways. A culture clash rose and remained for years. Aside from the culture divide, the Indian children seemed physically unable to sit and concentrate for the length of time required to learn in these schools. Government sponsored schools failed one after another.

Underneath the culture war between the whites and the Seminoles was the residue of the three military wars when the whites had been determined to destroy or remove the Seminoles from Florida. The Seminoles never gave in nor did they ever sign a peace treaty with the whites. The residue was the hurt, anguish and anger the Seminole men felt for the white men. And maybe gender was part of the problem. Maybe this was an issue between the men.

The new reservation contained well built dwellings, a medical facility, a school and other buildings, and government agent Lucien Spencer offered these to the Seminoles as a better place to live and send their children to school. No, they would not come. Frustrated, agent Spencer turned to Ivy Stranahan who had a friendly relationship with some Seminoles. He knew that she, along with her friends from the Daughters of the Revolutionary War, and the Fort Lauderdale Woman's Club, had financed Tony Tommie's entrance to the white school system. Spencer succeeded with their help, and after the first Seminoles moved to the reservation, others began to follow.

This happened because Ivy Stranahan and Annie Tommie were friends. This friendship, along with Ivy's straight-forwardness, created an historic scene that answered agent Spencer's dilemma. It went something like this:

On a beautiful morning in June, 1924, Ivy parked her Model T 600 feet from the front gate of the Seminole encampment. She had already done a lot of talking to them, including to Annie, of course, about what this new place would mean to them. It would be a genuine new beginning. She would help it happen. Now, Ivy wondered, and probably prayed, they would come. And slowly they did. Annie Tommie led the group of four into the Model T, and they rode away to the new reservation. Once they got there, Ivy got out, showed them the place, and they all started settling in, with Ivy's help that she continued to give at least once a week to make sure everything was going right. The Oceolas, the Tommies and the Jumpers had made the most important first step to make their world and the white man's world work together. Without the friendship of these two women, Annie Tommie and Ivy Stranahan, current history between these two proud peoples might be very different today.

Funeral Services Conducted For Seminole Medicine Woman

Funeral services for 90-year-old Annie Tommie, once a Seminole medicine woman, were typical of the changing of the Semoniles of South Florida, numbers of whom still refuse to accept the benefits of the Indian Reservations provided by the government. Of her six living children, only three attended her last rites, performed at the Dania Indian Reservation following services at the First Seminole Baptist Church nearby, conducted by the Rev. Stanley Smith, Indian missionary.

Actually it was extraordinary that any of Annie's close relatives should see her burial, and an indication of changing customs, for in strict Seminole tradition no close member of the family would approach the body after death, although four days of mourning is observed. But since her daughter, Annie, and sons, Frank and Sam, all of Dania, have embraced the Baptist faith, half of her children and many of her grandchildren who live at the Reservation, were there. Ben and Brownie Tommie, Dania, and Jack Tommie, Ft. Pierce, stayed stoically away. They observed the old Seminole custom.

Preceded By Sons

Two sons preceded the Seminole woman in death. Tony Tommie and Little Doc, both colorful figures in Broward's early history. Annie was born in 1856, eight miles south of the present Reservation, in Horsehead Hammock. She leaves more than 55 grandchildren and great-grandchildren, of which 10 attend school. One son is studying to be a missionary.

The crude little church was filled with Indians and white friends, for Annie was beloved by her tribe and consulted by whites. It was she and a brother, Willie Jumper, who were instrumental in moving Seminoles from what is now the West Side Ball Park to the Reservation. Her childhood days were spent near Coolee Ham-

mock, now an exclusive residential district.

Modern Funeral

There were flowers, the usual prayers and obsequies, and a modern funeral home directing proceedings, but one of the old Seminole habits was continued. Annie's tribal costumes and household goods, even the tall walking cane she carried for years, were placed in her coffin and buried with her.

Funeral services for Seminoles not living on reservations, like those on the Tamiami Trail, are very different. The corpse is taken by friends deep into the Everglades, placed on the ground with all its worldly possessions, covered with palmetto branches, and surrounded with a sort of fence.

When the Reverend Smith presided at Annie's services, he related that Annie had accepted the White Man's God three months ago, in the presence of another Indian missionary, Rev. Willie King. Jose Billy, Seminole Indian who was a former medicine man but who is studying for missionary work at Lakeland, made a Seminole prayer.

King, located now at the Brighton Reservation, spoke in Seminole tongue of the life of Annie. It must have been touching, for there was weeping among the Seminoles there. Among mourners were two daughters of Annie's sister, Lena Huff Billie, and Alice Huff Billie, whom Annie had raised.

Pall bearers were Billie Osceola, Junior Buster, Dick Bowers, and Bill Osceola. She was laid to rest among the 107 graves of Seminoles. As last words were said, an airplane flew over, another mark of changes taking place in Annie's 90 years.

ANNIE TOMMIE — Her influence with the Seminole tribes brought defiant chieftains and their families into the government reservation west of Dania. Her life bridged the gap between the days when tribes hid out in the Everglades to today when 10 of her 55 grandchildren and great-grandchildren are receiving formal education. [Photo by Kelcy.]

Obituary for Annie Tommie. Her friendship with Ivy Stranahan linked the whites and Seminoles in such a way that it benefitted the Seminole nation and led to their successful enterprise today called the Seminole Hard Rock Casino and Cafe.

Annie Tommie's character was as strong as Ivy's. Perhaps, that's why they developed their friendship. Annie Jumper was a Creek. She married Doctor Tommie, a Mikasuki. That alone would make her unusual and unique. She crossed tribal lines in this marriage. The languages of both these tribes are very different. That meant she and her husband became bi-lingual. That meant both would bridge two different tribes with their linguistic abilities. Gradually, trust between them and leaders of the two tribes emerged. With trust came, a certain power and the position of leadership. Both Annie and her husband assumed that role. Tony Tommie probably was tri-lingual, learning the language of his two parents' tribes, plus English. Tony became the first Seminole to attend and succeed in white man's school. He and his brothers assumed leadership roles as the relationship between the Seminoles and the whites began to improve.

In her obituary, the news story revealed that three month's prior to her death, Annie had accepted the white man's God in the presence of an Indian missionary, Rev. Willie King. That made the funeral services for her quite unique and unusual. Even in her death, Annie had brought together the two previous warring factions: the white men and the Seminoles. Her services were at the First Seminole Baptist Church and conducted by Rev. Stanley Smith. The 12/27/46 *Fort Lauderdale Daily News* article stated:

> *"Actually it was extraordinary that any of Annie's close relatives should see her burial, and an indication of changing customs, for in strict Seminole tradition no close member of the family would approach the body after death, although four days of mourning is observed. But since her daughter, Annie, and sons, Frank and Sam, all of Dania, have embraced the Baptist faith, half of her children and many of her grandchildren who live at the Reservation, were there. Ben and Brownie Tommie, Dania, and Jack Tommie, Ft.Pierce, stayed stoically away. They observed the old Seminole custom.*
>
> *There were flowers, the usual prayers and obsequies, and a modern funeral home directing proceedings, but one of the old Seminole habits was continued. Annie's tribal costumes and household goods, even the tall walking cane she carried for years, were placed in her coffin and buried with her.*
>
> *Pall bearers were Billie Osceola, Junior Buster, Dick Bowers, and Bill Osceola. She was laid to rest among the 107 graves of the*

Seminoles. As last words were said, an airplane flew over, another mark of changes taking place in Annie's 90 years."

As the plane flew over Annie Tommie's funeral, it was a reminder of the early days when flying was in its infancy in Fort Lauderdale. The 1920s hosted a new era for transportation in Fort Lauderdale. Lorna Simpson, a reporter and pilot, wrote a history of Fort Lauderdale aviation history on which this narrative is based. She painted this picture of the era:

"These were the days when barnstormers, independent outfits, and infant flying schools blossomed forth all over the Miami area, when what are now the substantial, established airlines of this vicinity were only fledglings—when there were flash-in-the pan and wild cat ideas of various colors circulated prospecting airlines to Cuba and the Southern Americas."[11]

Affluent and adventurous citizens bought their own planes and housed them in town. One outstanding pilot, Merle L Fogg, perhaps, an early snowbird, had come to town from the skies of Maine. He enthusiastically joined the other sky hoppers and became part of the aviation scene in town. When the men got together, they wished for an airport, flying schools, and all their parts to make aviation not just a dream but the dream of a business. For all of their talk, nothing more happened. Until one day.

Merle Fogg took off that Tuesday in early 1928 for a routine flight. Later that afternoon, people learned his plane had crashed in Huffman's orange grove near West Palm Beach. Fogg was found dead. The reaction of the people of Fort Lauderdale showed how much they admired and loved this flyboy. All the disconnected pie in the sky talk about an airport and landing fields, all the pie in the sky talk suddenly turned into action. The golf links named for the railroad hero, Henry Flagler, became the site of the airfield. It would be a memorial to Fogg and named for him. Even before an airfield started, an emergency landing strip was cleared by December of that year. Finally, all the aviation talkers became an association of aviators. The next year, in May, the Merle L.Fogg Memorial Airport hosted 5,000 townspeople who came with heavy hearts to honor Fogg but were pleased how a tragedy had turned into a celebration of the aviator they all loved.

The Merle L. Fogg Memorial Airport covered 180 acres which became the Naval Air Station in 1935, and after the War became the International Airport. In 1936, two important events occurred at the airfield. Pilot Annette Gipson arrived to break her previous record of height flying. When she flew her plane to 12,628 feet, she succeeded in breaking her former record. The other important visitor that remained to advance the airport was the Works Progress Administration. Under the WPA, an aviation ground school and model training school filled important spots at the airport.

Now, enter Lorna Simpson, a writer, educator and pilot. Another Fort Lauderdale resident, she became a pilot and a member of WASP (Women's Airforce Service Pilots).

Lorna Simpson (1908-1995)

When she arrived in Fort Lauderdale with her family in 1923, a genuine cold spell hit town and choked the outside spigots of her neighbor's house. Not put off by that cold front, Lorna stepped up and began to serve the community by using her graduate degree from Stetson University. She began as a reporter and feature writer of the *Fort Lauderdale News* and *Sun Record*. Not only did she report but she also became a writer for a children's nature show that aired on TV station WGBS. The show "Pelican's Pouch" taught children the unique value of the nature around them and how to care for nature in a Christian, loving way. This show put her in the historic forefront of early TV shows aimed for children. But Lorna had a bent for education which she eventually used when she became a pilot in the WASP.

In the early part of World War II, the Women's Airforce Service Pilots (WASP) were women pilots who ferried newly made airplanes to the front lines of war. Some categorized their work as simply conveying cargo or supplies. Not so. Each aircraft had to be transported one at a time to where it was needed. This meant the WASP missions were often dangerous and put these pilots in harms way. The WASP story has been captured in a documentary film called "Fly Girls". As a member of the WASP, Lorna became part of an elite group of women who ferried aircraft, tested planes, instructed male pilots, and towed targets for anti-aircraft practice. Between 1942 and 1944, about 1,000 women were recruited. They flew 60 million miles, and 38 were killed in the line of duty. An interesting story about the B-29 plane shows the importance of the WASP. With its history of engine fires, that plane needed boosters to convince men to pilot it. Two women were recruited to fly it and to show it was safe. They proved the B-29 was safe "even for a woman to pilot." The B-29 went on into history as the *Enola Gay* that housed and dropped the atomic bomb.

Lorna made aviation education into her life's work. She soloed with Tony Piper who ran a flying school here in Fort Lauderdale. She received her Student Pilot Certificate in May, 1939 and began her climb to master aviation skills. In August, 1940 she gained a Private Pilot Certificate. Then when she achieved her Commercial Pilot Certificate in September, 1941, she became the first woman in Broward County with that distinction. Still reaching, she made Instructor Rating on the Commercial Certificate, the

This one and only picture of Lorna Simpson is from the newspaper Evening Sentinel, *Sunday, June 21, 1941, superimposed over the Ft. Lauderdale International Airport when it was an Airforce base.*   Files at Hoch Center

second woman in Broward County with that achievement. She spoke of harrowing and dangerous experiences flying into storms when there were no sophisticated instruments to guide her.

Continuing in aviation, she taught ground school for Ted Thompson at the Fort Lauderdale airport. With five ground ratings in navigation, meteorology, CAR, engines and aircraft in 1942, she became a teacher of cadets in ground school at the University of Miami. At this same time that she became a WASP she also continued to teach Piper Cub flyers, the club operated by the Piper Club factory for employees who wished to learn to fly.

Too Hot To Hide

Lorna had advanced so that she had her own ground school. After she married in 1944, she maintained two planes which she used for cross county flights. Like Katy Rawls she joined the Ninety-Nines, the national women's flight organization founded in 1929.

We don't know much about Lorna's personal life, but we know she was a very unusual woman to have achieved such a high mastery of aviation at a time when that was a very unusual skill for a woman to acquire. Not only was she an intelligent and a gifted teacher, but she was brave and bold to fly before high technology in aviation was available to guide her.

The other Fort Lauderdale resident and member of the WASP was Katherine Rawls. Her name is on the first plaque of the historical walkway in Stranahan Park and so is actually number one on my Women's Walking Tour. She certainly was an historic figure "Too Hot to Hide" and a star for Fort Lauderdale.

Katherine Louise Rawls (1918-1982)

Out of the dark days of the great Depression of the 1920s and 30s in Fort Lauderdale came a star. A prodigy of the water, precocious, petite, Katy Rawls as a youngster began to break swimming and diving records the likes of which had not been matched at that time. As a swimmer and a diver at the 1936 Olympics in Hitler's Nazi Germany, she captured two silver medals and one bronze. She might have garnered more but some competitions were held at the same time others were. Since she could not be in two places at one time, she had to pick the ones in which she would compete. She performed when most folks did not know about little Fort Lauderdale, a beach town in Florida. Where was that? Well, through Katy, people actually began to go to a map to locate this place called Fort Lauderdale.

In 1935, her swimming accomplishments launched the beginning of the College Swim Forum which eventually developed into a world class swimming facility now known as the International Swimming Hall of Fame in Fort Lauderdale. The Forum sought swimmers from the many college campuses to compete but also to learn in a clinic setting, the only one of its kind in the country. The fact that Katy was such a swimming star here made Fort Lauderdale a natural choice for college swimmers especially during their winter break time.

In 1965 Katy was inducted in the International Swimming Hall of Fame along with Johnny Weismuller, Buster Crabbe and Don Schollander. During her life, Katy garnered the National Swimming Championship and won the National Diving Championship 26 times. An exhibit of Katy's swimming career is on display at the International Swimming Hall of Fame museum today.

The Rawls family came to Fort Lauderdale in 1934 from Nashville, Tennessee. All five Rawls children were swimmers. Many of them competed and broke records. But Katy won more and more often. When asked how she became involved in swimming, she replied words to the effect that money was scarce in those early days. There was always the pool and she could swim free if she joined the swimming team. And so she did. Swimming turned her life into a great adventure. As a young star competitor, she toured many cities in America and eventually the world.

PROCLAMATION

WHEREAS, Katherine Rawls is the world's all-time greatest aquatic
performer; and

WHEREAS, Katherine Rawls won innumerable championships, titles,
medals and honors in both swimming and diving throughout her career; and

WHEREAS, Katherine Rawls considers Fort Lauderdale to be her
"home town;" and

WHEREAS, Fort Lauderdale wishes to show its pride in having
Katherine Rawls, the world's greatest woman swimmer,
as one of its most distinguished citizens; and

WHEREAS, I, VIRGINIA S. YOUNG, Mayor of Fort Lauderdale, Florida
do proclaim January 28, 1974, as

KATHERINE RAWLS DAY

NOW, THEREFORE, you are invited to attend a reception in honor
of Katherine Rawls on the top floor of Fort Lauderdale's
City Hall from 5:00 p.m. to 6:30 p.m., Monday, January 28,
1974.

Fort Lauderdale's mayor, Virginia Young, proclaimed January 28, 1974 as
Katherine Rawl's Day and issued an invitation to a reception honoring Katherine.
Files at Hoch Center, Fort Lauderdale Historical Society

Seemingly unruffled or distracted by the excitement of her competitions
and with extraordinary skill and stamina, she won many contests as a
teenager. In 1937 the Associated Sports Poll named her the best woman
athlete in America. She won over such notables as Babe Dedrikson, Patty
Berg, Alice Marble, and Eleanor Holm. Katy was then only 19 years old.

A spectacular photo of Katy Rawls in full readiness to swim.
Photo from the International Swimming Hall of Fame

Too Hot To Hide

World War II cancelled the Olympic Games, and so Katy turned to a new love: aviation. With her husband Tom Thompson, who owned a flying school, Katy learned to fly and secured her pilot's license. She joined the WASP, along with Lorna Simpson, who we met in the previous chapter. Of the original 25 members on this experimental team, these two women represented Fort Lauderdale. Eventually there were 1,000 women who flew planes over the Atlantic. WASP later morphed into the Women's Air Force. With her second husband also a pilot, Katy traveled to Saudi Arabia where he consulted with the aviators about their air force and Katy gave swimming lessons to Prince Faisal, then a youngster. Back in America, Katy became a swimming instructor at various clubs in Florida and West Virginia.

In 1974 Fort Lauderdale's Mayor Virginia Young declared January 28 as Katherine Rawls day.

Cancer claimed Katy when she was 64 years old.

Buck Dawson, in his book about the International Swimming Hall of Fame, wrote this sentence in his biography of Katherine Rawls:

"The best reason for the Swimming Hall of Fame being in Fort Lauderdale is Katy Rawls." He went on to say that she was "...the girl who started it all."[12] Her high profile accomplishments as a young woman made her a natural celebrity. Moreover, she carried that crown with grace and good humor.

Because of her outstanding swimming and diving records, Katy put Fort Lauderdale on the map. Equally so, her remarkable swimming and diving victories stimulated the reason for a swimming hall of fame to exist at all and especially in Fort Lauderdale. Her achievements reached beyond herself personally...into her hometown and into the sports of swimming and diving. Katy Rawls left an indelible legacy in the water history of Fort Lauderdale and America.

My time at the International Swimming Hall of Fame also included a talk with Bob Dunckle, Executive Director. I asked Bob who else I should include in my book about outstanding women swimmers. He answered rather quickly, "Stella Taylor."

Stella Taylor (1930-2003)

As her name translates, Stella was a star. But you wouldn't know that at first glance. She was pudgy, not tall, certainly not trim nor slim in her build, but that face, crested by yellow hair held those remarkable eyes that not only sparkled but searched the outside world, her outside world of swimming, of marathon swimming. Not a flashy swimmer but Stella's windmill strokes of 72 a minute, even with a faulty left stroke, turned her into a swimmer of extraordinary stamina. Even though she was an older swimmer, she broke world records. As such, she brought honor particularly to the sport of swimming but also to Fort Lauderdale and to those local swimmers who adopted her, supported her, and cheered her on.

Stella began swimming when she was 33 years old. According to her, she chose swimming as her life's work after a romantic experience did not come out well. She began to swim at the International Swimming Hall of Fame. She swam so much, so long, so often that the staff began to notice her. From my own experiences with swimming, it is a very sensual sport. Surrounded, in a sense, by as much water outside of the body as there is in the body gives one a sense of comfort and joy. It is among the few sports than a person can do solo or with a team. Stella became at one with the water. A look at her earlier life would show the possibilities of her transformation into a marathon swimmer. She had honed a tolerance for discomfort and yes, even pain. That tolerance turned into the stamina and endurance necessary for marathon swimming.

Born in Bristol, England, Stella became an elementary school teacher. When she came to America in 1958, she entered a convent to become a sister of God in Buffalo, New York. That religious life did not suit her, and she reentered the outside world, looking for herself. What should she be? When she came to Fort Lauderdale, she became a teacher of handicapped children. When her affair of the heart did not turn out well, swimming became her focus—serious swimming.

Swimming became her life. She said, "I live in a tiny apartment in Fort Lauderdale. I don't really have any clothes. And my gear is about to fall apart." When she accomplished a marathon swim in Lake George, New York, she explained her views about marathon swimming in a 1981 interview published in the *Evening Times*:

Too Hot To Hide

Stella Taylor put on full face make-up before swimming, ready for the press when she emerged victorious from the water.
International Swimming Hall of Fame photo

"Marathon swimming makes a person unfit to live with. But the feeling of accomplishment you get is worth all the praying, all the pain and all the suffering. When I accomplish my goal, I'm happy for all the people who helped me as I am for myself."

The International Swimming Hall of Fame inducted her as one of its own stars in 1994.

At the age of 45, Stella's spectacular swim of Lake George brought high attention to this woman who swam on grease and guts. She braved the 41-mile swim in water that rocked with four- to five-foot waves and a north wind that never ceased during her 26 hours and 51 minutes in the water. She beat the former record of 31 hours and 27 minutes. She was the oldest woman to accomplish that feat and the second woman who ever swam Lake George. Surrounded by Fort Lauderdale supporters, including Bob Dunckle, now Executive Director of the ISHF, she took inspiration when she viewed her two favorite teddy bears perched high on the pole of the support boat that accompanied her. Her trainer Jack Nelson told her to swim like a tiger and she did.

Stella was courageous. During her victorious swim of Lake Okeechobee, the Florida Games and Conservation observer counted over 100 alligators in the water at the same time. As the oldest woman to try it, she swam the English Channel twice. There was something about being an older woman swimmer that pushed Stella on. Her swims in Loch Ness, Scotland; Everglades City, Florida; in the Atlantic Ocean Gulf Stream; and Lake George hit headline news and brought Fort Lauderdale into the limelight. At the ISHF pool in 1982 she broke the Guinness record for swimming time in a pool.

Stella was a natural with press people and she served as a special goodwill ambassador wherever she swam. The press dubbed her the swimming nun and others described her as a petite version of Joan Rivers. Marion Washburn, the librarian at the Henning Library knew Stella and worked with her many times. She said she had a bubbling personality and was especially engaging in teaching children at the pool.

Without any family here, the people who knew her at the International Swimming Hall of Fame behaved like her family. In retirement, Stella returned to teaching at the Fort Lauderdale Oral School, Coral Ridge County Club, Nova High School, and the ISHF. At 72, she died at the Sisters of Mercy Convent of complications from a brain tumor. But in her death, as in her swimming, Stella needed help from her friends in Fort Lauderdale. And they did not fail her. There was no money for her funeral or her resting place. The City Commissioners provided Stella Taylor, their marathon swimming star, with a place in Lauderdale Memorial Park.

In that Park, a giant Florida Oak tree umbrellas the place where Stella lies buried. The marble bench over her gravesite shows at first glance her name "Stella Taylor," but the sitting place chronicles her victories:

Guinness Book of Records for CROSSING ENGLISH CHANNEL
OLDEST WOMAN *1975-1994*

Atlantic Ocean Gulf Stream	*51 hours*
Hall of Fame Pool	*65 hours*
Lake George, N.Y.	*Loch Ness, Scotland*
Lake Okeechobee, Fla.	*Everglades City, Fla.*

KEY TO THE CITY OF FORT LAUDERDALE

| *Dec. 19, 1930* | *Feb. 11, 2003* |
| *Bristol, England* | *Fort Lauderdale, Florida* |

This intrepid English woman called Stella Taylor who wondered where she belonged, found a welcoming home in Fort Lauderdale and in the sport of marathon swimming. Her swimming accomplishments brought honor and recognition to Fort Lauderdale, to the International Swimming Hall of Fame and to marathon swimming. With tenacity and courage, she broke swimming records set by people younger than herself. She proved how determination could beat the clock even when it was set against you.

Too Hot To Hide

She lived up to her name . . . star.

Just as Stella Taylor took her life straight into the victory of marathon swimming, Sylvia Aldridge looked at Fort Lauderdale when she came here and paved her way into history. She saw it as a place that was segregated. But she did not take that history and shake it up. Instead she worked with it and saw some business opportunities that would benefit both whites and blacks. Her response was nothing short of brilliant and innovative.

Sylvia Hill Aldridge (1884-1962)

Sylvia Aldridge and her husband Anderson moved from Gainesville in 1906 to Fort Lauderdale. She arrived at the beginning. The black community at that time consisted of seven homes and two stores.

Sylvia Hill was the sixth of 11 Hill children from a black family unusually affluent for that time. The family owned 1800 acres inherited from their forebears who became freed slaves after the Civil War. We don't know about her schooling, but we do know from her behavior that Sylvia Hill Aldridge was a very unusual woman. She had a rare talent for observation of what was or was not around her. This capacity made her a leader in her community. Once here, she soon saw there were many jobs available. She quickly landed a job as a housecleaner-maid for a white family. Soon she noticed that many white families needed domestic help, and she also noticed many black women needed jobs and did not know how to find them. It seemed logical for Sylvia to start an employment agency from her home. Then when she noticed her maids had trouble with transportation, she started Sylvia's Victory Cab, guaranteed to get the maids to work on time. She became Fort Lauderdale's first black woman entrepreneur.

She not only matched black women with white families; she also taught her maids how to clean and keep a white house well. She provided sparkling white uniforms for her maids. She listened to any complaints from her white families about her maids. She straightened those complaints out promptly. Her management skills crafted a necessary and successful business.

When one thinks about

Sylvia Aldridge, the first African-American woman entrepreneur in Fort Lauderdale, was also very involved in her community. Courtesy Broward County History Center

Too Hot To Hide

Sylvia's business, it was innovative and certainly an "out of the box" solution. Women in those days, especially African-American women, spent their working out-of-the-house time as domestic helpers. But Sylvia took that concept and packaged it into a business. When she started her taxi business, well, didn't that idea turn your head around? She was an ingenious businesswoman, one of a kind.

The Aldridges created a good living for themselves. They ran a small restaurant from the side of their house. They rented out property they owned. Their son George died tragically. He was found murdered and the perpetrators of this act have never been found.

In 1936 when a truck loaded with farm laborers overturned, some black workers were killed and there was no place to treat the wounded. Helpers laid the injured men out on the lawn in front of whites-only Memorial Hospital. Sylvia Aldridge, who tended to the men as well as she

This photograph of the African-American children picking vegetables in the fields reminds us that until 1946 these children received only 7 months a year of schooling until a federal lawsuit proclaimed their right to 9 months of schooling.
FLHS archives

could, saw immediately that her community needed a black hospital. With her participation and the help of others who fundraised for two years, the first black hospital, Provident Hospital, emerged. Ivy Stranahan took part in her effort. Provident remained as the only black hospital until the 1960's when desegregation opened the white hospitals to black patients.

Sylvia's philanthropy knew few bounds. She donated land for the sanctuary of her church, St. John's United Methodist. She was trustee and benefactor of Bethune-Cookman College in Daytona. She was a member of the Northwest Federated Women's Club, the American Woodsmen, the NAACP, Eastern Star, Heroines of Jericho, and the Grand Union of Pallbearers. After she died, many tried to save her house for history but it was destroyed in a fire.

Sylvia Aldridge, Fort Lauderdale's first African-American woman entrepreneur, became firmly planted in her community. Her astute business sense created businesses to help black women, particularly, find work in the white world across the tracks. Some called her a Good Samaritan and others regarded her as an angel. So many remember her with her trademark response to a request or need, "Baby, I'll get right to it". She must have said that with a twinkle in her eye.

World War II came upon Florida waters as early as 1939 when the United States was still neutral. One well-known episode included a British cruiser, *Orion*, which fired two shots off the bow of the German freighter *Arauca*. To avoid further attack from the *Orion*, the freighter raced into Port Everglades. Meanwhile, the *Orion* kept vigil to trap the *Arauca* if she attempted to escape to the open seas. Once in port, the freighter, unable to unload its cargo, suffered several thousands of libels because of non-delivery of goods. Fort Lauderdale authorities interned the captain and 42 crewmembers until 1941. Why did that happen?

President Roosevelt often visited Florida to go fishing. On one such trip down here, he saw the *Arauca* birthed and proudly flying the German flag. Quite angered by that scene, he ordered the Coast Guard to seize the ship, jail the crew, and hoist the stars and stripes over the *Arauca*.

During the War, the threat of German submarines off the coast kept the military on its toes. Armed men patrolled the beaches of Broward County towns blacked out during the nights. Military and civilians manned towers

Too Hot To Hide

In 1936 President Roosevelt, like other presidents, found fishing in the Fort Lauderdale area a pleasure and diversion from his duties at the White House. In town again in 1939, he ordered the docked German ship Arauca stripped of its German flag which was replaced with the stars and stripes, and then directed the crew to be jailed. Later, his administration would leave its mark in south Florida with the WPA and the CCC programs of the New Deal.   FLHS archives

to eyeball the coastal waters for submarines. The Navy took over the Merle Fogg Airfield as well as most of the seaport facilities to store munitions and supplies. Port Everglades became a Naval base which turned itself over for wartime use. A special project even included carrier pigeons. In order not to use the routine messenger routes which could be intercepted by the Germans, the pigeons transported those important words safely. The waters off the coast remained hostage until August 1942.

A participant of the fight that destroyed the German wolfpack gave his story. As we know, the wait of fighting folks in anticipation of a battle, is often frustrating and tedious. That was true here. The sailors wanted action. Soon that changed. Once the cluster of German submarines became known, every ship, every single plane in the area converged on that site and destroyed the wolfpack. That victory certainly dismissed their boredom. The coast was ours again.

When the War ended in 1945, Fort Lauderdale and Port Everglades pulsed with an unprecedented spurt in growth. The soldiers and sailors formerly stationed down here went home and many turned around and came back to Fort Lauderdale to settle down. The Port benefitted from the new usage of container shipping perfected during wartime. Only now, during peacetime, container shipping changed the ways of moving goods around the world. This whole new industry born during wartime now pressed into service for peacetime.

The United States benefitted mightily from the War. In the War, it was the only country involved that suffered no damage to its land or its economy. On the contrary, the Depression before the War now turned into an economic boom. What also changed was the transformation of the status of three minorities in our society. All wars changed the places where women worked. Shortages in domestic employment happened when men left their jobs at home to fight in that war, or any war. To fill this vacuum, women stepped into the workplaces where men once performed. This pulled them out of their niche, the kitchen, the home, into out-of-the-house work. During World War II, this change in women's and minorities' workplace was dramatic and unprecedented in our history. The great need to fill these shortages in employment also affected Black Americans and gays. Looking at the steps leading to the women's movement, the Civil Rights movement and the gay rights movement in the 1960s, one can clearly see those steps as they happened during WWII and thereafter. The rumblings of a social revolution began during WWII.

Some early steps into the Civil Rights movement began in 1937 when Clarence and Frances Macon Walker came to Fort Lauderdale and brought sunshine to the education of African-American students. At that time African-American children attended school only seven months of the year, from Autumn to Easter. From Easter to Autumn, children aged seven and older picked vegetables in the fields. White children went to school for nine months. That was school board policy.

As principal of Dillard School, Mr. Walker advocated for Dillard to receive school accreditation which could only be achieved if the school year was nine months long. In July, 1941, the same month that celebrated American independence, Principal Walker organized a student boycott. Black students would not pick vegetables in the fields and would only show

Too Hot To Hide

up to attend school in September like the white children. That year, the school board relented and established a nine-month school year at Dillard. But that decision did not hold.

The next year, the school board reversed its decision based on pressure from white farmers who needed cheap labor to harvest vegetables. Already plagued with ill health, Principal Walker pleaded with the school board to recant its reversal. Unmoved, they refused. That night, fatigued by the fruitless meeting, he suffered a heart attack and by the morning or July 8, 1942 had passed away. His successor, S. Meredith Mosley, followed Walker's strategy of the boycott. That summer, the farmers faced empty fields again, and in September the students arrived en masse at Dillard. For four years the struggle carried on until 1946, when a federal court decision *Clarence C. Walker Civic League et al v Board of Public Instruction for Broward County* returned Dillard School to a nine month school year. Clarence Walker had finally won his case. During Mosley's tenure, which ended in 1969, Dillard School won its first accreditation by the Southern Association for Schools and Colleges. Although Clarence Walker pushed his educational agenda, he was acutely aware of the cultural temper of Fort Lauderdale. He left us these words:

> *"Let us join hands in training the Negro youth to have respect for Fort Lauderdale, for idealism, for lawful obedience, for faithful service, for building up civic pride and friendship between the races."[13]*

Just about the same time as the Walkers came to Fort Lauderdale, another woman, Eula Gandy Johnson, also came to town. You might say, when Mrs. Johnson came to Fort Lauderdale, she turned it upside down.

Eula Gandy Johnson (1914-2001)

Sometimes one meets someone in history, someone who was in the right place at the right time to do something incredibly right. One could say that about Eula Johnson. Her story of civil rights activism showed her to be the right person to do it. Some called her Fort Lauderdale's Rosa Parks. Eula Johnson's challenges aimed at many areas. Her high profile demonstrations and unrelenting pressure to achieve racial equality for the blacks put her at the front line of the war between the blacks and whites in Fort Lauderdale. Her posture was pure bravery in view of the threats she received, the attempted bribes, arrests, law suits and the head-on confrontations with the police.

Eula Johnson was a black Joan of Arc.

As a fair skinned black woman, Eula Gandy was not that "black." She could have stood by and passed for white, thereby relieving herself of hardship and pain. But she did not take that route. Even as a nine-year-old in Georgia, she had begun to feel the burden of being black. The story goes that she refused to enter the side door, the entrance designated for blacks, of a place where she went to get gasoline. Instead, she stood solidly at the front door until she got what she wanted. For her entire life, she adamantly refused to enter by the back door or the side door. She insisted on entering only by the front door. Remarkably, at only nine years old, she already had an image of herself as a worthy citizen, not a second class black girl, but just like everyone else regardless of color.

Mrs. Johnson was the seventh of ten children in a Georgia family. She moved to Fort Lauderdale in 1935. She owned a gas station and raised her three children. When she arrived here, she made the following observations of the status of blacks:

- Blacks could not cross the railroad tracks after 8 pm.
- The only blacks allowed on the beaches were those who were employees.
- Blacks were not allowed in white restaurants.
- Blacks were not allowed in white hotels.
- At the bus station, blacks were crowded into one corner.
- On the bus, blacks had to sit in the back.

Too Hot To Hide

- Blacks could not use restrooms in downtown stores.
- Blacks could not go to white parks or swimming pools.
- Blacks could drink water only from colored drinking fountains.
- At the Courthouse, blacks could not use the elevators.
- The colored high school went no higher than 10th grade.
- Blacks could not vote in local elections but could in national elections.

After awhile, Eula Johnson thought that much needed to be changed in Fort Lauderdale and set about doing just that. Her most impressive work came when she achieved the Presidency of the National Association of the Advancement of Colored People (NAACP) in town. While this act marked her as the first woman to head this prestigious organization, her talents of organizing and leading culminated in her rise to this post. She honed these skills and used them to achieve some groundbreaking challenges to the white establishment in Fort Lauderdale. As President of the NAACP from 1959 to 1967 she led her charges against discrimination in the following places and ways:

- On July 4, 1961, she along with others conducted the first wade-in at a Fort Lauderdale Beach.
- On August 7, 1961, she along with others staged the second wade-in.
- In 1961, several other wade-ins at the beach occurred.
- The City of Fort Lauderdale sued Mrs. Johnson for inciting chaos and being a public nuisance. A Federal Judge ruled in her favor and against the segregated beaches.
- Nine years later, in 1970, Fort Lauderdale beaches became desegregated.
- She organized picket lines protesting segregation at the drive-in movie.
- She led eat-ins at lunch counters and sit-ins at the bus station.
- She organized picket lines at Southern Bell, Florida Power and Light Company, local supermarkets and department stores that refused to hire black employees.

This remarkable woman seemed unflappable to the response of threats from the white community. With great tenacity and courage, she stood her ground and was very clear that she was right in what she was doing. She was brave. Often challenged by authorities who questioned her motives she would respond with words to the effect that God was guiding her in her

This picture of Eula Johnson et al says so much about her. She is dressed all in white. Is that an accident? I think not. She's made a statement about blacks and whites. Her expression says, "Don't mess with me, I am determined." She is marching in City Hall. That picture is her signature image that graced the cover of the ribbon cutting ceremony program on July 4, 2011 (next page). The ceremony opened Eula Johnson's house as the new office of the NAACP in Fort Lauderdale.
Fort Lauderdale Historical Society

CENTENNIAL WADE-IN COMMEMORATION

MONDAY, JULY 4, 2011

Join the City of Fort Lauderdale and the Fort Lauderdale/Broward Branch of the NAACP to celebrate the opening of the restored Eula Johnson House and commemorate the 50th Anniversary of the historic Wade-In that led to the integration of Fort Lauderdale Beach.

RIBBON-CUTTING CEREMONY
AT THE EULA JOHNSON HOUSE

9:00 a.m. | 1100 NW 6th Street | Fort Lauderdale, FL 33311

BEACH WADE-IN CEREMONY

and unveiling of a State Historic Marker
11:00 a.m. | A1A and Las Olas Blvd. | Fort Lauderdale, FL 33316

MIDTOWN COMMERCE CENTER RECEPTION

1:00 p.m. | 1033 NW 6th Street | Fort Lauderdale, FL 33311

Eula Johnson's house, now the new NAACP office.
The crowd at the ribbon cutting on July 4, 2011.
Author's photo

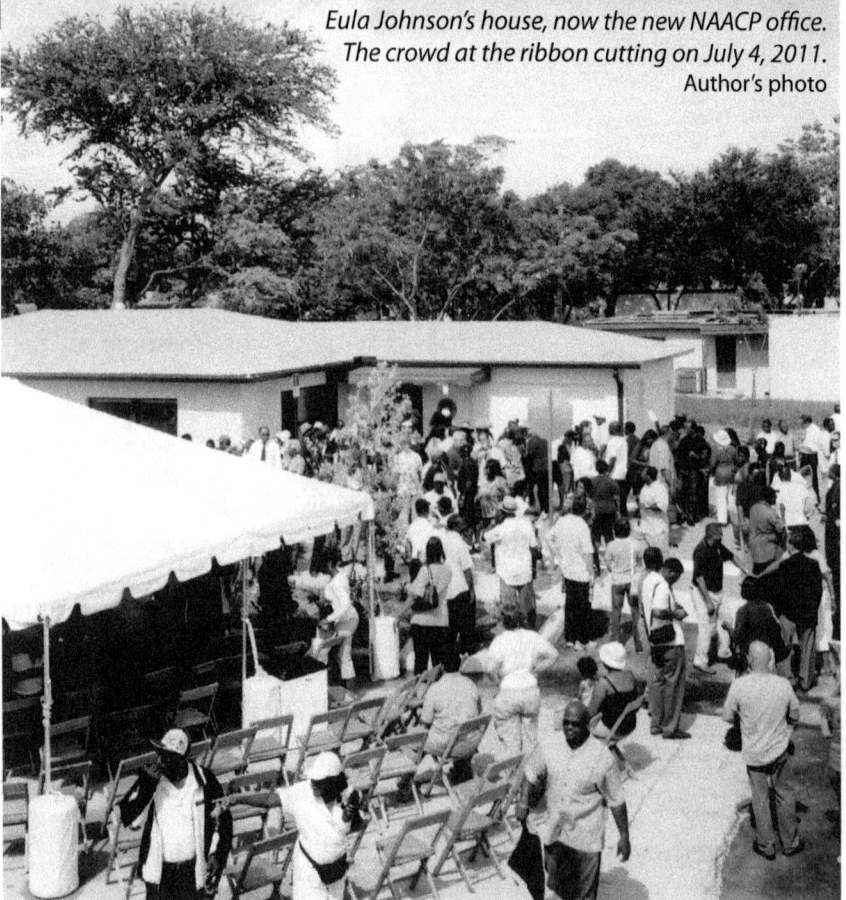

Too Hot To Hide

quest of racial equality—and that He was right. It seemed clear that she felt she was under His protection and she had little to fear. Such determined convictions, it would seem, left little to dispute.

In her struggles, Mrs. Johnson revealed she had help from her white sisters and brothers. And at times she criticized other black leaders from sitting out on this struggle. Her quest for racial equality benefited both the white and black community of Fort Lauderdale and made it what it is today. In her later years, she received honors from the Alpha Kappa Alpha sorority, the Broward Branch of Christians and Jews, NAACP, and the Kathleen Wright Bridge Award from the Urban League of Broward County. None of this discourse can be finished before reminding readers how great her influence was on the actions of others, black and white, in Fort Lauderdale. She encouraged others to think beyond themselves to the benefit of Fort Lauderdale. As such, Mrs. Johnson's footprints in Fort Lauderdale history are legendary.

I attended a joyous, really jubilant, event the morning of July 4, 2011, when the city officials, members of the City Centennial Committee and the NAACP hosted a ribbon-cutting ceremony that transformed Eula Johnson's modest house into the headquarters of the NAACP. On July 4, 1961, exactly 50 years to the day, Eula Johnson had led the African-Americans' wade-in at Fort Lauderdale's "white" beach. Today's July 4, 2011 celebration happened at 1100 NW 6th Street, Sistruck Ave. Greg Johnson, grandson to Mrs. Johnson, was at the '61 wade-in, and reminisced about that day and his life with his grandmother. He said he cried that day at the wade-in and his grandmother chastised him. Likely, as a child he felt the danger and tension that many remember about that day. He was often scared for her. She got "those phone calls." She had a journey to take, and she was going to it. She sued everybody in town. When he said that, the audience laughed knowingly. He thanked everyone for coming out.

Marsha Ellison, president of the NAACP, spoke about how dangerous Johnson's work was. The planning committee had to meet in secret. Their work was uncompromising even when some in their own community did not support their efforts. She felt that Mrs. Johnson's love of God pressed her forward and gave her courage.

Later that day, the "wade-in" enactment at the beach included the unveiling of an historic plaque commemorating the 1961 march to the ocean that triggered many other challenges of the Civil Rights movement in Fort Lauderdale. Also, these two events that day not only celebrated the Fourth of July but the Centennial of Fort Lauderdale.

As the Civil Rights movement charged into Fort Lauderdale, changing events affected the lives of women in the Native American community. Betty Mae Tiger Jumper was another woman whose life Ivy Stranahan touched. Although she was alive at the time I began my research I was told she had Alzheimer's condition. I felt it best not to try to reach her as there was so much material about her that I could use without speaking to her. During the time of my research and writing, she passed on.

Betty Mae Tiger Jumper (1923-2011)

"Do not let hardships stand in your way. Set small goals and work towards them, even if it's only 15 minutes a day." —Betty Mae Tiger Jumper

It is daunting to write about a woman who is clearly a legendary figure. It gives one a reason to pause and think hard about what words to use. While Dr. Betty Mae Tiger Jumper is called a community activist, she based her actions on her vision of what she perceived were the needs in the English- and Seminole-speaking cultures in this part of Florida. She defined herself as a bridge between Native Americans and white Americans. She pushed herself to master the English language and became a translator between the peoples of these two races. When she became versed enough in both cultures, she found the best in each to share with the other. In doing so, she generated actions to benefit each, and as she performed this service, repeatedly, her reputation for honesty and truthfulness grew. Her acceptance by both races gave her a spiritual renewal that provoked more actions on behalf of each to the other. She accomplished this when the relations between the Native Americans and the Americans were still tense and untrusting.

Betty Mae Tiger's hardships began as soon as she was born. She was half white and half Seminole. According to the rules of the Tribe, she should have been drowned at birth. But her family saved her. Her helpers were some Seminoles who had converted to Christianity and thereby were at odds with such Seminole beliefs. Not only was Betty half white American but also Christian. However, in her common sense wisdom, she knew she was also half Seminole. She never forgot that. Her command of such sensitivity throughout her life pushed her far beyond what she could ever have imagined as a child.

To keep the child and her family safe, relatives of the Snake Clan moved five-year-old Betty to Dania from the Indiantown area. But that change did not guard her from the name-calling she and her brother Howard endured from the Seminole children there. Betty became very outspoken about such verbal abuse and reacted. When she met Ivy Stranahan, who was a founder of the Friends of the Seminoles, she was drawn to her message of gentility and learning. She became convinced that educating herself must

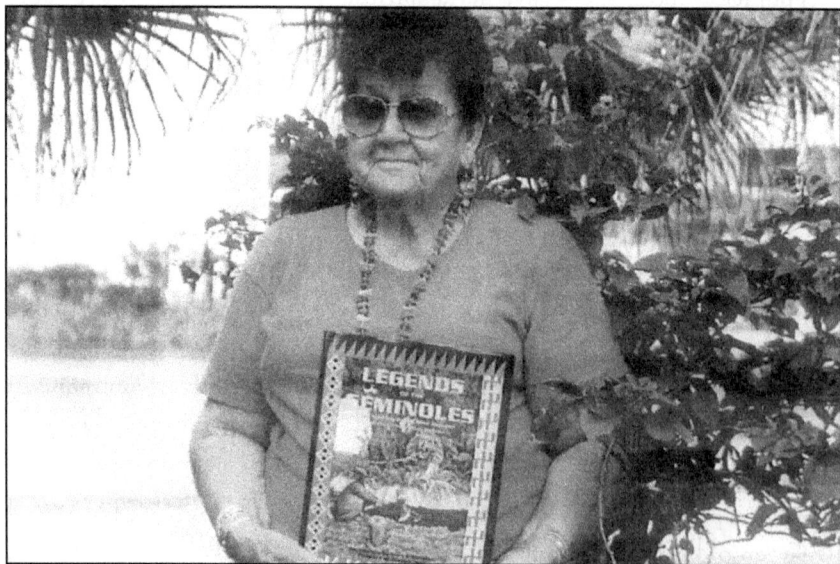

Betty Mae Tiger Jumper embodied the belief that education will make you free and open doors to places that had never been opened before. Her early leadership forged the bridge between the Seminoles and the whites in Fort Lauderdale. Inspired and at times supported by Ivy Stranahan and the Friends of the Seminoles, she achieved what no one else had done before . . . success for the Seminole people.

FLHS

Too Hot To Hide

be her number one goal. Blocked from acceptance to the local white school and the black school, Betty, her brother Howard and their cousin Ann Parker chose to attend the Quaker Cherokee Boarding School in North Carolina. Some of her relatives feared that such a close connection to white Americans might turn her away from her Seminole roots. She recalled that one of the hardest changes of attitude she had to learn was looking straight into the eye of a stranger. Such behavior was against the Seminole way. However, she was with the Quakers, whose expansive views on life meant that education will open the doors of the world to all who embrace it. Such precepts, without prejudice, had provoked the Philadelphia Quakers to produce, in 1683, the first written proclamation against slavery in the New World.

Following Betty at Cherokee, 21 Florida Seminole children enrolled until 1947 when Broward County School Board admitted Seminole children to public schools. Betty paved the way and others followed.

When Betty came home during the summers, she found herself requested to interpret for the Seminoles, particularly in medical situations. She spoke both languages of the Seminole tribe. It seemed reasonable that Betty Mae would study medicine, so even before she finished high school, her aspirations were publicly known. After graduation from Cherokee, Betty trained to become a health field worker by attending the Kiowa Teaching Hospital in Lawton, Oklahoma. In 1945 Betty returned to Florida's Jackson Memorial Hospital for a year as an interpreter for Native American patients and medical staff. Finally, with funding secured, Betty and another trained health worker began their rounds

Betty Mae Tiger Jumper, Seminole leader

By Anthony Man
STAFF WRITER

Betty Mae Tiger Jumper, who became the only woman to lead the Seminole Tribal Council, died at her home Friday. She was 88.

Tribal officials and her family also believe she was the first Seminole Indian to graduate from high school. Born in Indiantown, she was unable to gain admission either to segregated schools for white or for black children, so she persuaded her mother to let her leave home for a North Carolina Indian boarding school, said her son, Moses Jumper Jr.

She received a high school diploma and returned home with training as a nurse to help start the Indian Health Program.

She led the Tribal Council in 1967-1971.

"Not only will our tribe feel the loss of Betty Mae, but so will all of humanity," said Mitchell Cypress, Seminole Tribe chairman.

Mrs. Jumper is the last surviving matriarch of the Snake Clan. She was preceded in death by her husband, Moses. She is survived by three children, Moses Jumper Jr., Scarlett Jumper-Young-Liebowitz, and Boettner Jumper; two brothers and one sister; nine grandchildren; and 36 great-grandchildren.

Visitation will be 10 to 11 a.m. Monday at House Of Prayer, 6200 Stirling Road, Hollywood. A service is at 11 a.m. Monday. Interment will be at the New Seminole Cemetery in Hollywood.

Betty Mae Tiger Jumper's obituary from the Sun Sentinel, *Jan. 16, 2011.*

administering at Seminole reservations in Dania and Tamiami Trial camps. She was back home at last.

When government funding for that position disappeared, Betty volunteered for seventeen years, from 1947 to 1964. The people she served gave her a new name, "Doctor Lady".

In 1953, Betty found herself in a new area of service.

The Federal Government determined that certain tribes would be mainstreamed into American culture and society. This meant tribes like the Seminoles would lose their tribal lands and reservations. On one level, this was a clever way to open more land for white Americans to settle while reducing government allocations for these reservation lands. The Seminoles had to be convinced it would be to their distinct advantage to insist on Federal Jurisdiction. As independent as they wanted to be, it would be in their beset interests to have their own land and not lose it. The challenge was two-fold: to organize those Seminoles against giving up their land and to convince the Federal authorities that the Seminoles needed their land. Once again, it was the U.S. government against the Seminoles. Betty Mae organized a response to this challenge. Ivy Stranahan and many Friends of the Seminoles also rose to oppose Federal takeover of Seminole lands. They won.

Betty became vice-chairman of the Florida's Seminole Tribal Council, newly organized in 1957. In 1966, she campaigned for the chair of the Council and won. She became the first and only woman to achieve such an elevated position in the Seminole Tribal Council. Her organizing skills held her high as she brought the Council's treasury from a meager $35 to a half million dollar surplus. She led the movement to form the Southeastern Tribes in 1968. UNSET members early saw a need for improved health care for their peoples, and their lobbying efforts paid off. The government responded in 1969 by establishing the National Council on Indian Opportunity, an idea from Richard M. Nixon, a Quaker, a presidential candidate and later the President of the United States.

In 1970 Betty traveled to Washington, D.C. to be sworn in for a two-year term as a member of the National Council. Months later, the National Seminar for American Women named Betty Mae Tiger Jumper as one of the "Top Indian Women" of the year. When she ran for reelection on the Tribal Council, she lost but continued her work on the reservation. However, now she had another new assignment: to speak and tell the story of the Seminoles. In 1994, she put her stories on the printed page and produced with Peter Gallagher the first Seminole book about their culture called, *Legends of the Seminoles*. Others are: *And with the Wagon—Came God's Word* (1985), and with Patsy West *A Seminole Legend: The Life of Betty Mae Tiger Jumper* (2001).

Her accolades continued to come: Florida Folk Heritage Award in 1994; Honorary Degree from Florida State University in 1995; the 1995 Woman of the Year award from the State of Florida; and the Native American Journalists Association's first Lifetime Achievement Award in 1997.

When Betty was a child, her grandmother Mary Tiger, gave her an Indian name. She called her, Pa-ta-kee, which means "Soldier". Betty Mae Tiger Jumper lived up to that name.

Another woman who would occupy a first, this time in city governance, was Easter Lily Gates. Known for her festively decorated hats, Mrs. Gates was our first woman supervisor of elections. How she got that job is her story.

Easter Lily Gates (1889-1985)

The life of Easter Lily Gates is the story of a widow, a single mother, who found work wherever she could to support herself, her two sons and her mother in the desperate times of the Great Depression and hurricane in 1926. As she found work, she provided historic firsts for women, for Fort Lauderdale and for Broward County: the employment she eventually found was Supervisor of Registration of Elections, she was the first woman to fill that political post, and she served in that post for 40 years, longer than any other person who served the county at that time.

Her name likely came from the day of her birth on Easter Sunday, April 21 in Des Moines, Iowa. After she married George Peter Gates in 1910, they moved through Utah, Nevada, and Pennsylvania before they decided to take Dr. Freiday's offer to farm some land he owned in the area where the Fort Lauderdale airport is today. The year was 1918 and the First World War was on. Her husband became a plumber and worked in Miami. Mrs. Gates raised chickens and turkeys and then planted citrus trees and sugar cane. During the boom real estate times of 1924, they sold that land and bought a place where the courthouse is today. Mr. Gates became progressively ill with anemia and died in 1926. Not only did the hurricane destroy all their property but the depression wiped out all their savings. Banks failed, money was scarce. Suddenly Mrs. Gates found

Re-Elect
EASTER LILY GATES
DEMOCRAT
SUPERVISOR
OF
REGISTRATION
Tuesday, Nov. 3, 1964
A Trusted Servant of Broward County
HONEST, COURTEOUS AND FAIR TREATMENT is accorded all who visit the office of Supervisor of Registration regardless of race, color, creed or affiliation. Anyone who has ever been in the office of EASTER L. GATES has received any information pertaining to the REGISTRATION RECORDS as provided by law in a POLITE AND CHEERFUL MANNER, REPUBLICAN AS WELL AS DEMOCRAT.
THERE IS NO SUBSTITUTE FOR EXPERIENCE
ATLANTIC PRINTING

Easter Lily's 1964 election promotion card.

FLHS files

Too Hot To Hide

herself with no husband and no money.

Easter Lily Gates had a tenacious hold on life. She had a lifelong habit of relating to people. She would do any kind of honest work. Her affiliations with the Masons and Eastern Star helped her in ways she could not imagine. In a 1982 interview she explained in detail how she handled her challenges. After the hurricane she lost everything and did not even have any clothing to wear. She said,

> "I can sympathize with those who are in need when they have to go through a thing like that because that's what I had to do. I had just been paid $20 and I put it in the bank. I then had $65 in the bank... But... "when I went down to the bank, the doors were closed. A crowd of people were around. There wasn't any use saying anything. I went home. The Lord's taken me through worse than this. I guess He's not going to desert me now.

> "At about 10:30 there was a knock on the door. It was a boy. 'I have some groceries for you.' I didn't order any. It must be for the people around the corner.

> "'No, this is for Mrs. Easter Lily Gates.' 'Well, I'm Easter Lily Gates.' He brought them in. There was a well rounded order of groceries. To this date, I don't have the least idea who that was. But, those groceries came.

> "I do know that the Lord answers prayer. He's answered time and again with me."[14]

Still looking for work, she met the Superintendent of Schools one day, and asked him if she could drive a school bus. First he said no, because no women drove school buses. Then it became a yes and she became the first woman school bus driver in the county, another first for Easter Lily Gates and another first for women in Fort Lauderdale.

School bus driving held her over for a while, but she really needed a job that paid more. Friends asked her how she was faring and she explained it that way. She had a family to support. Friends suggested she run for Supervisor of Elections. So "I looked into it, saw it was something I could do."[15] She began on the Election Board for some special school elections. She read laws from the books. With experience and reading, she satisfied herself that she could do the job and proceeded to run for office. She had

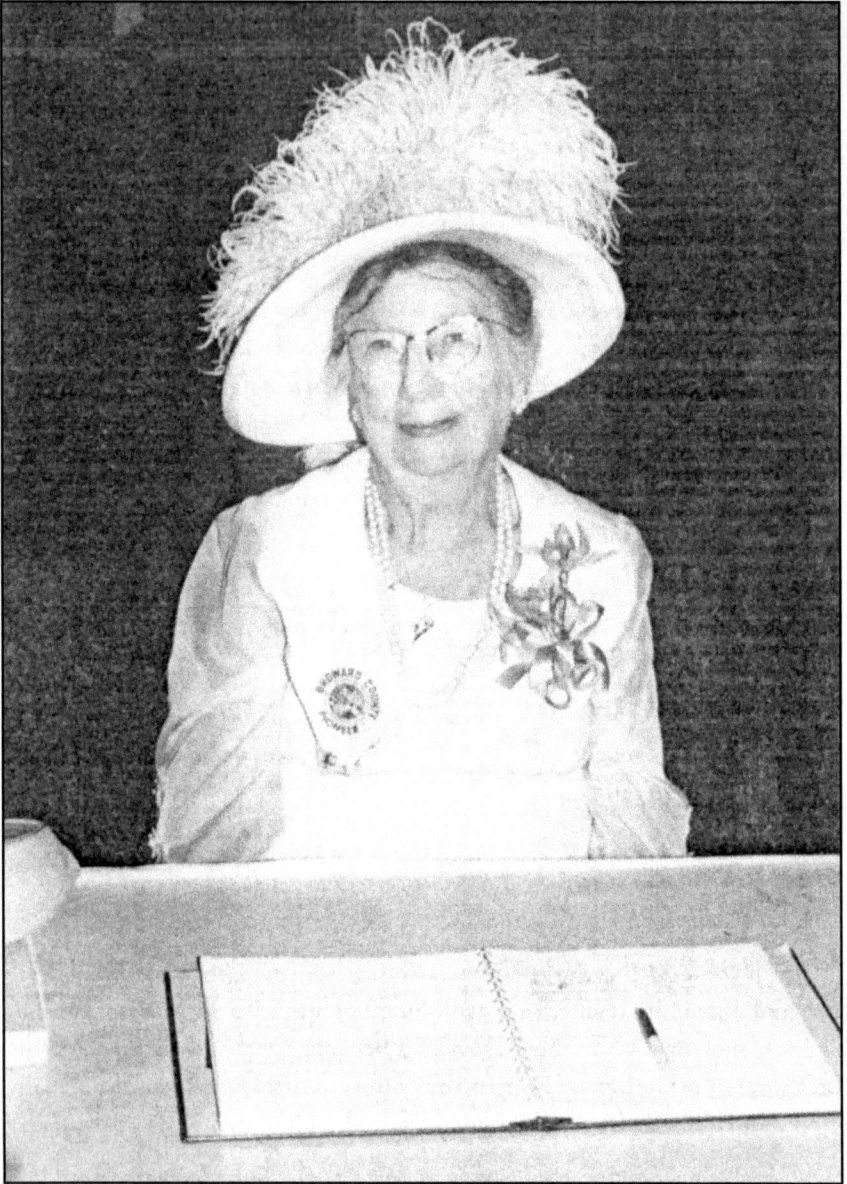

Easter Lily Gates, Fort Lauderdale's first woman registrar of voters, wore her festive hats on many occasions.   FLHS archives

cards printed for her election and gave them to voters. Men often told her she should be home like other women. She explained she'd like that but her husband had passed away and she had to support two boys and her mother. They liked her straight talk and passed the word on to other men.

Close-up of one of Easter Lily's hats.   Author's photo

She won the election.

She explained the rugged hours she put in to accomplish her job. "I was on duty from Tuesday 'til Friday morning, at 9:00.

> *"It was always 39 hours, at least, that I'd be on that job. I didn't have any sleep at all during that time because they'd be coming in at all different hours on Tuesday night and the next day. After the ballots came in, I'd go to an evening prayer and then go on home.*

> *"When I had all my work finished, I'd certify it to the Secretary of State and send the returns up there. I'd have to go the post office to do that.*

> *"In the 1948 election, that was so long, it was Friday morning before I got off. All the sleep I got during that time was five hours."*

Easter Lily registered the first Native Americans in the county to vote and went to the African American community to engage them to vote as well. She registered the first non-white voters in the history of the county. She directly pursued her position as Registrar of Voters to encourage all who were qualified to vote regardless of political party affiliations or color of skin.

Many people in the county remembered and recognized Easter Lily Gates as a lady who wore large, pretty hats. Below that pretty hat was the head and heart of a woman who pioneered the first county post held by a woman with dignity, honesty, and just plain common sense. She completed her county time in 1968 and passed on in 1985.

Another woman who was a first in city governance was Florence C. Hardy who defined the position of city clerk and then became the first woman to hold that position. A park at 25 SW 9th Street, now enjoying an expansion, is named for her.

Florence C. Hardy (1897-1975)

In her lifetime Florence Hardy received many awards for her outstanding service to the city. She became the town's first city clerk when that office did not exist. She developed the office and thereby became the first woman to hold that post in Fort Lauderdale. As city clerk she became the keeper of the keys to the city's records, the city's governmental history.

After her retirement in 1963, she became the second president of the Fort Lauderdale Historical Society and assisted in the Stranahan Foundation duties. The Society became the recipient of many records Mrs. Hardy provided, and historical researchers like me have much to thank Florence Hardy for.

The Hardys were Broward County pioneers. They arrived in 1924. William Hardy came here because he was ill and hoped that Florida would benefit his health. He was known as "Doc" since he ran the town's Rexall Drug Store, which he sold during World War II to the Breeding Drug Company. For the next 17 years he became the State Beverage Agent.

Although her college education was limited to classes at Brown and later at University of Florida, Florence Hardy had an outstanding knack for organizing materials and managing them in an orderly way. When she developed the city's clerk position in 1957, that was only one of many civic posts she held. She had been City Auditor, 1927-29; Assistant City Manager, 1928; Acting Personnel Director, 1946-51; and Executive Assistant to the City Commissioner, 1955.

She knew where the records were. She knew how to answer questions with those records. That talent proved invaluable to all who worked with her. She was cool, calm, collected, capable and reliable. Those attributes helped Fort Lauderdale's city government grow responsibly. Her friends at City Hall knew this and honored her with a plaque. That plaque became of interest to me. I wanted to find it. After trying several places, I found it in the special collections department of the Fort Lauderdale Historical Society's Hoch Center. It was sitting in a drawer. A letter in her file stated that the Fort Lauderdale Historical Society would honor Mrs. Hardy by mounting her plaque on its premises. This is a beautiful plaque that should be mounted so we can honor her accomplishments for the city as well as

SONG OF BROWARD
By Bruno Schmidt
(*Fort Lauderdale News*, May 12, 1968)

HISTORICAL LADY

A building stands in Holiday Park
    In shades of palm and pine,
As a noteworthy, true landmark
    In Lauderale's design.
Within this modern structure,
    The Historical Society
Preserves its by-gone culture
    For now and time to be.
If we should pass its portal
    And browse within a while,
Our memory will be immortal
    Of a lady with a smile.
She is the Society's President
    With salary that isn't;
And all her hours that are spent
    Are given in good will.
Her name is Florence C. Hardy,
    And William is her mate;
They came in nineteen twenty-four
    Good life to anticipate.
She was for almost two scores
    Of years our City Clerk,
But lucky for our Society,
    She chose for us to work.
God must have been especially kind
    To lend Florence His grace,
Which kindles in her thoughtful mind
    And lights her friendly face.
Historians may long refer
    To friends of yours and mine.
But our City named a Park for her
    As a Florence C. Hardy shrine.
So may her full historic life
    Re-echo God's own voice:
"Consultant, mother, friend or wife—
    You are my angels' choice!"

the Fort Lauderdale Historical Society. The plaque still sits in a drawer.

In the business community she also served and received awards. The Business and Professional Women's Club gave her its first prestigious award. Rotary, Kiwanis and the Rosicrusians also honored her.

"Our Florence" passed on almost one year after her husband. Her great legacies to us are her collections of Fort Lauderdale's governmental history which she kept carefully and lovingly. In 1963, the year she retired, a park was named in her honor.

As the women's movement took hold throughout the United States, women began to push up on the glass political roof and become mayors, senators and congresswomen. Virginia Young became one of these super stars.

Commissioners of Fort Lauderdale named a park in Florence Hardy's honor to reward her for many years of outstanding work as guardian of the city's records. She was our first city clerk. (inset) Florence Hardy. Author's photo; Inset from FLHS

Virginia Shuman Young (1917-1994)

At the receiving desk of the Virginia Shuman Young Elementary School, Dr. Strauss the principal told me that if I went to the eighth floor of City Hall, there I would see pictures of all the mayors of Fort Lauderdale, and there I would see Virginia Shuman Young's face looking back at me, the first and only woman mayor of Fort Lauderdale. She was mayor twice, in nonconsecutive terms.

In her book *Mangrove Roots of Fort Lauderdale*,[16] written with Gretchen Thompson, she presented the history of Fort Lauderdale through her eyes, growing up in it and instrumental in its progress. While most of the book tells Fort Lauderdale's story, Mayor Young's personal philosophy shines through. She explains her life as if she were rehearsing all those early years to become officially the city's mayor. She felt the town's ups and downs.

When recalling how she came to Florida from Virginia, where she was born, this is how she characterized those years in the third person:

> *"Four-year-olds often think bigger than life of monsters and dinosaurs yet, if this four-year-old could have dreamed reality, she would not have been able to dream large enough. A half century later she was to become the first woman mayor of the fastest growing city in the nation, the city she was going to visit now with its Indians and mosquitoes, sandroads and tents—a city like no other in the entire country."*

Little Virginia, likely named for her native state, thrilled to stories from both her father and grandfather about the black bears and turkeys they killed so the family could eat, learning how to swim by falling off a boat in Lake Okeechobee, talking to the Native Americans when things got lonely, and how to make a noise like an alligator. Her family jumped right into the early government and became friends with the early politicians of the city and state, putting Fort Lauderdale first, of course. Thanks to these stories, Mayor Young learned to love early Florida.

The 1920's posed even larger problems and challenges than those she heard as a child. After the first World War, Fort Lauderdale boomed. Optimistic changes had improved the conditions of the town. Coming to live in Fort Lauderdale in 1926, she remembered, "When we arrived, it was boom time and butter and eggs and everything were all so expensive that we really had to be frugal."

"But even then I knew this was the place to be. It was a new land, exciting dreams and people filled with enthusiasm.

"It was at this time that the Northern Banks were getting worried about their customers who were borrowing money to put into Florida land. There had been earlier land sales and some of them had been underwater.

"Anyway, the banks began putting pressure on their borrowers, and by 1926, this pressure was being felt in town. Things were slowing up with a lot of plans being postponed. The hand-writing was on the wall—for anyone who wanted to read it—about some sort of economic slow-down."

Then Mother Nature joined the problems and sent two hurricanes in 1926 and 1928 that left Fort Lauderdale with very little intact. Martial law was declared. Mayor Young recalled,

"...my birthday was Sept. 16. I'd gotten a piece of rose silk. I always

Virginia Young's portrait as it hangs in the elementary school named for her.

FLHS files

wanted rose silk for a dress and my mother and grandmother promised they would make me one from the piece of material.

"The wind started blowing the night of my birthday. I remember waking up and hearing my Dad say he thought we were going to have a hurricane.... It was a stormy night and the sky was red before it got dark. When we got up the next morning it was an angry red and the wind was howling.

"Anyway, when we woke up it was all solid water outside, and the water kept coming up and up...mother took Blanche who was then six weeks old and sat her on a tall chifferobe [sic]. The rest of us climbed on chairs and tables....then dad took the closet door off the hinges, a narrow one, and nailed a dresser drawer on it so it would float easily. He put rubber sheeting in the drawer and floated Blanche in that. The door knob was sticking up and he made Irving, and Myra (then 1 1/2) and me put on our bathing suits and tied a rope around our waists. Then he tied the rope to the door knob.

"He was trying to make us as safe as he could if the house floated off the foundation. And it did just that. I was only nine and I was worried, but the thing I was worried most about was my rose silk dress."

They survived, all of them.

"We ate canned soup, drinking it out of the can. Nobody had anything at all....We lost everything, People didn't have any money. The banks were wrecked. So were the grocery stores...just about everything was in ruins. Everyone helped everyone else.

"We learned a lot from the boom and the hurricane...we learned not to build frame houses just sitting on foundation blocks...those properly anchored had no trouble. We learned hurricanes are to be feared and protected against and this was the birth of the South Florida Building Code.

"Today some people look down on builders and developers, but I don't. It was the developers who drained the land and got rid of the mosquitoes, sandflies, sandspurs, and palmettos. After the hurricane of 1926 we learned the true meaning of self-sufficiency and that is why I believe those after 1926 are the real pioneers."

The boom that busted and the disasters of the hurricanes made 1929 as a year that people lost fortunes. Some lost it all. "We still aren't in paradise yet, but we have the dream."

While everyone did not have jobs, people had little gardens and grew enough food to sustain themselves. These lean years did not mean that young Virginia, ready to graduate to college, would go to college. The family money went to her brothers for higher education. Undaunted, she went to work, and her combined work and volunteer experiences paved the way for her entrance into politics. Ginnie, her nickname, became a doer. Whatever the problem, she grabbed it by the handle and shook it until a solution came out. She joined just about every committee in town and usually became its president. It made sense for her to become mayor. She tried twice and made it the third time. Then she made mayor twice, first in 1973-75 and again in 1981-85.

She forged some other first woman positions:

• first woman to chair the school board
• first woman elected president of the Florida League of Cities
• first woman director of a bank

From the business world of her family-owned construction company, it was no secret she wanted to see Fort Lauderdale grow. She made herself a representative of Fort Lauderdale much like its chief publicist. When Lauderdale's own tennis star Chris Evert played in England, Mayor Young stood in the stands and cheered. Behind her cheerleading attitude, Mayor Young exhibited outstanding executive ability and tough-mindedness that sometimes met with criticism. But that did not stop her if she felt she was right. She said so and stood hard and fast.

While her work and her volunteering catapulted her into public office, it was clearly Virginia Shuman Young's character and the spirit she brought to those experiences that made her an obvious candidate for city leadership. One can see these qualities in how she portrayed her struggles through some tough times in the 1920's. She knew what do to with what she had and used that philosophy in public service.

Virginia Shuman Young was undoubtedly Fort Lauderdale's first lady.

Another important movement that often is associated with women is the preservation movement. Actually begun as early as the efforts to preserve Mount Vernon by the Mount Vernon Ladies Association in 1853, the movement gained momentum in the 1950s sometimes as a reaction against the Redevelopment Agency programs sponsored by the Federal government. Its object was to clear cities of slums and build new housing. Sometimes, the definition of a "slum" differed depending on one's perspective. Women, particularly, have made an important impact in preservation, in that often they see houses or buildings as worthy of preservation or renovation to be later used as historic sites, museums etc. Because a woman's "office" is her house, she has a special feeling for a house that is definitely hers. A house is a woman's dominion. Therefore, some old houses slated for demolition have met resistance mostly from women who want to save them.

For instance, the story of the saving of Mount Vernon, the house of our first president, was a feminine one. The house was ready to hit the dust. No one wanted it. Women asked the government for help. Nothing came of the request. Exhausted from asking for help, women, particularly Ann Pamela Cunningham, of South Carolina, organized a fundraiser that saved Mt. Vernon when no one else wanted to. She asked two affluent women from each state to contribute to the effort, and that started the saving of Mount Vernon. To this day most people think Mt. Vernon is managed by the Park Service. No, ma'am, just lady volunteers. Bonnet House is a local example of a house kept alive by the lady's preservation attitude and program.

Evelyn Fortune Lilly Bartlett Huber
(1887-1997)

"I don't want this place to change. I hope it will continue".

Evelyn F. Bartlett

As Evelyn Bartlett said this of her Bonnet House, she passed on the stewardship of the 20 room house and its 35 acres of grounds in Fort Lauderdale to the Florida Trust for Historic Preservation in 1983. This act put her in the company of the many women preservationists.

In her lifetime, she had three estates to manage: a house in Beverly, Massachusetts; the Bothway Farm in Essex, Massachusetts; and Bonnet House. Perhaps telling of her awareness of time-management concerns, she stopped her painting (1932-1938) when they bought Bothway Farm which was described as large. No doubt developers approached her to buy Bonnet House or part of its grounds. However, she had her own vision of Bonnet House and its land. She understood its place in time and aimed to preserve it that way. When I visited Bonnet House, turned the car into the parking lot surrounded by foliage and trees and got out, I quickly became aware of a presence. Although I never knew old Florida, I had read about its aura, and when I walked to the reception cottage, I felt I was back in old Florida. These grounds originally part of what is now Birch Park across Sunrise Highway, stand together as a separate preserve but caught in the beginning excitement of the 20th century while expressing its early Florida era.

Behind Mrs. Bartlett's quiet, reserved demeanor was a person with artistic intensity. She painted what was around her in bold, exuberant and joyous colors: plants, animals, personal possessions, and then, with her extraordinary eye, she portrayed family members. She and her husband covered Bonnet House, inside and out, with whimsical decorations and drawings. They stroked ceilings, floors, doors and walls with their fine, carefree but articulated touches. Sunshine yellows and passionate blues predominantly cover the house. Bonnet House emerged as a beach house with a sense of humor.

Mrs. Bartlett gave aesthetic attention to the details of everyday living

Evelyn Bartlett with her dog and pet monkey.   Bonnet House archives.
1986 Distinguished Citizen Award plaque to Evelyn Bartlett on the side of Fort Lauderdale City Hall.   Photo by author

DISTINGUISHED CITIZEN AWARD
1986

EVELYN F. BARTLETT

FOR HER BENEVOLENT SUPPORT OF
THE EXPANSION AND PRESERVATION
OF FORT LAUDERDALE BEACH

Bonnet House.
Photo by author

A rustic terrain with a rugged naturalness seemingly from early Florida surrounds Bonnet House and provides a contrast to its sophisticated splendor.

Author's photo

and turned them into rituals of a gracious lifestyle. Each day's menu was served with style and dedication to its importance in creating a timeless intensity of daily living. As if company was coming each day, the meals themselves became the "company" of the day and were presented with her exquisite china, crystal and silver. Hers was a life less of what she said but how and what she did at Bonnet House each day.

Her management style became a seamless connection of all the staff with her and her husband. On-site support staff wrote very affectionately of the Bartletts, claiming they felt more like a family than paid employees. The interrelationship of the Bartletts and their staff helpers became as one as they regarded the place and each other with affection and respect. One might say that Evelyn Bartlett's management style was clear but gentle. Such talent and skill are often dismissed as expected of one with such wealth, especially if she is a woman. But actually, the management skills necessary to run a small house or large house are too frequently underestimated and women managers too often forgotten as crucial to successful living and preservation.

If one wanted to guess where Evelyn Bartlett learned how to manage, one might look to her father, William Bartlett (1863-1942), a self-made millionaire who was a whiz at turning failing businesses into financial successes. In Indianapolis, he headed nine telephone companies and became a director on the Eli Lilly board. Local public organizations like the Red Cross turned to him for improvements. He accepted such requests and changed failures into successes. As a Lilly director he supplied aircraft to fly medical aid to needy communities from 1925 to 1927. From sparse records of their early life together, one can only speculate that Evelyn Bartlett learned about management from her father. Then when he offered, she learned how to paint from her husband who honed his talent in Germany and with James Abbott McNeill Whistler in Paris.

Arriving as Frederic Bartlett's bride in 1931, she described Fort Lauderdale as "just a village" still recovering from the hurricane of 1926 and the devastation of the Great Depression. They supported a staff with the management of Bonnet House and grounds during this economic downturn. But the support was reciprocal. They needed work and the Bartletts needed people to make Bonnet House work.

Some might regard Evelyn Bartlett as just a rich lady, but such a view

Too Hot To Hide

would miss her great contribution to preservation in this day and age when too often buildings and places are obliterated in the name of "progress." A visit to Bonnet House can give one a very special view of this great lady and take you back to a time when graciousness ruled the tempo of the day.

The Bartletts had a special relationship with their property keepers who were African-Americans and whose life in the 1930s and '40s at Bonnet House was memorable to them. The Bartletts and their employees shared a reciprocal tenderness. They lived together in a special world altogether different from the segregated environment that surrounded them. The Bartletts sensed the pain of their employees' segregated life in town. Incorporating them as their family, they shielded them from the racially divided world outside of Bonnet House. Outside was a different story.

The Civil Rights movement pressed the educational system for reform. The Federal Court mandated that schools must be desegregated. Parents in many towns and cities became angry and anxious. At times, white parents moved away from places where such changes had to be made. The object of the legislation was to insure equal educational programs to both African-American and white children. White and black children together would attend schools. Separate but equal was no longer satisfactory. Now, enter into this a young woman who seemed absolutely right for the job in town.

Kathleen Cooper Wright (1936-1985)

Kathleen Cooper Wright spent eight years of her public life as the first African-American on the Broward County Board of Education. Those other years she taught social studies at Dillard High School. During her tenure on the Board, she continued to teach and also attended graduate school for her doctorate in education, which she received from Nova in 1980. That she could accomplish these three tasks when she also was a mother and wife said a great deal about her executive ability.

Elected to the Board in 1973, she won the seat of Vice-Chairman the following year. As Vice-Chair, she requested at her first Board meeting that the Superintendent present a report on the desegregation of public schools in Broward County. There she was at the historic time of school desegregation. Was it a coincidence that she, the first African-American, was elected to the Board at that time? Was it an accident that she ran for that office at that time? I doubt it. As a social studies teacher, she knew it was time to correct an inequity for the students in Broward County. Did she know at one time African-American students attended school only seven months out of the year so that they could spend two months picking vegetables in the fields? Aware of these and other inequities, she was there to make changes that would bring about quality education for all children regardless of color.

Kathleen Cooper was born, raised and educated in Fort Lauderdale. She was one of eleven children born to Bahamian parents. At Dillard School she graduated as valedictorian. She returned to Dillard as a social studies teacher. From my reading of the minutes of the Board of Education from 1973 to 1981, I could say Mrs. Wright hardly ever missed a school board meeting. By February of 1975, she suggested a social studies class called "School and Community Service." Here one could see how her academic background spread into the community by creating a hands-on service in the place where the students lived. She wanted students to see and feel this connection she believed in. Her posture on the Board during these tense years of bussing and desegregation was best called conciliatory or, as the students would say today in their language...Mrs. Wright was "cool." She never wavered about desegregation. The minutes of the March 20, 1975 meeting recorded her position: "She felt that bussing was the only way to achieve integration." A few days later, she advised Board Members with words to this effect: "Don't

Too Hot To Hide

get into personalities and get too emotional about it."

Further into 1975, a teachers' strike occurred. Her advice to the Board members in October was this: "If PERC wants to go on and do what it feels it has to do, let them to it without drawing us in or trying to keep us in conflict." PERC was the Public Employees Relations Committee. That November, Mrs. Wright stood for Chairman of the Board but received votes only for the Vice-Chairman position. However, the following November, 1976, she became Chairman of the Board again. At the November 16 meeting she said the following:

> "I simply would like to extend my appreciation to my colleagues for their vote of confidence in asking me to serve as Chairman of this Board. In the past two years I have had the pleasure of working with a very fine group of persons, and in spite of the differences that many of us have had, I think that Board made some significant contributions to the school system. I certainly hope that the group of persons assembled here will continue to move forward in terms of providing strong leadership to this system.

> "I also want to indicate that leadership must be shared. Those of you who are seated here all assume a posture of leadership in terms of charting the direction for this school system. I want you to know that nothing that I do can be accomplished without your support and without your cooperation.

> "I would like to say to you that in paraphrasing some of the words that Abraham Lincoln said in his Gettysburg Address is that people will very soon forget the things we say here, but they will long remember the things that we do here. I hope that this Board will be a Board of action, one that will be positive yet calm, show a great deal of firmness but yet be compassionate.

> "I urge the support of the administration, the faculty and staffs in the centers across this county, and citizens of this community to work together in helping to make this the best system in the county. Thank you."

In 1977, Mrs. Wright lost that position. She resumed her post as Vice-Chair in 1979. The next year, Mrs. Wright earned her doctorate and remained a Board member until November 1982 when she resigned.

Kathleen Cooper Wright
Photo courtesy Broward County Historical Commission, *Hollywood Sun-Tattler* Collection

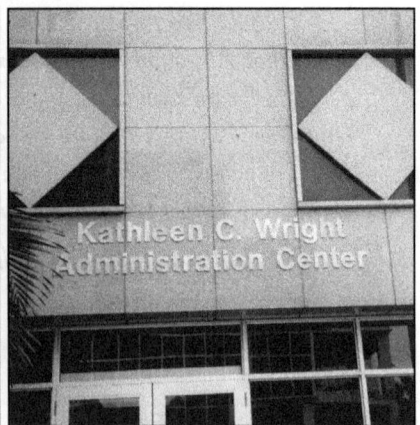

To honor her untimely demise, the county board of education renamed its building the Kathleen C. Wright Administration Center; the street bordering it was also renamed in her honor.   Author's photo

During her last years of her tenure, she consistently voted against the many student suspensions put before the Board. She voiced concerns that these troubled children needed the help that school staff could give. Turning them away would deprive them of the assistance they needed.

The minutes of November 4, 1982 recorded Dr. Wright's closing comments to the Board. She referred to her eight years on the Board as enjoyable experiences with colleagues despite differences. She knew there would be frustrating challenges due to reduction of school funding and the closing of some schools. She hoped all Board members would keep foremost in mind that the prime consideration should always be for the children. She said that while some Board decisions made it appear that members were uncaring, she knew that they would not be on the Board if they did not care about the children. Dr. Wright remarked that she hoped her absence from the Board would not result in the absence of concern for issues relating to the minority community.

During her time on the Board, school closures and redefining school boundaries were handled in relation to the court ordered desegregation. These were hot issues. Parents, teachers, and students were not happy, at times, with Board decisions. From the many people I know in politics, all have said that school board positions are considered the most difficult, the most emotional, of all political posts. Dr. Wright thought herself now ready for another political position. After she ran for a state senate seat and lost, she planned to run again. But that was not meant to be.

On her way to a conference in August, 1985, the plane Dr. Wright was on crashed and although she survived the crash, she passed away two weeks later at the age of 49. As a tribute to her legacy, the Board of Education renamed the Broward County School Board Administration Building the Kathleen C. Wright Administration Building in 1987. A street bordering the Building also was renamed in her honor. Efforts begun in 1998 to raise her memorial statue at the Building are at this time pending.

Anne Kolb (1932-1981)

Some might have called her Broward County's Joan of Arc, wielding her pen against the endless stream of developers eager to build where no one should build if one had any appreciation of the fragility of the land. But they didn't. The press dubbed her Broward County's first lady. Anne Kolb clearly turned county government inside out.

She came here in 1954 from St. Louis and slowly began a career in journalism that turned her into a muckraker who doggedly pursued a story until she got to the bottom and then wrote it to the top. She took a very serious view of how government worked or didn't. Her journalism awards covered issues about tuberculosis, reckless driving, hospital costs and treatment of African-Americans. In her article criticizing Broward County government, she described the system as "topsy-turvy" and a "bureaucratic octopus". Her writing that demanded the Pollution Control Board become an accountable defender of the environment earned her an appointment to the County Pollution Control Board. After two years, she resigned that post and ran for the County Commission. November, 1974, she became the first woman in history to win a seat on the Broward County Commission.

Anne Kolb: 1932-1981

Aside from her acute nose for news, Anne was a botanist, a lover of Florida's flora and fauna, and a devotee of the land and its natural beauty. She became a protector of the land and used her political arm to challenge the moneyed fingers that reached out to develop and develop and develop. Once they got the land, she lamented, they did not know how to care for it. So the descriptions of her from those she challenged included words like: blunt, caustic and sharp-tongued. She encouraged school children to be honest and speak out. She

Too Hot To Hide

said, "My personal philosophy is that people who manage the money control the world. Women have a lot of money, but generally they don't manage it well. We need to change that..."

Two years into her post as a County Commissioner she successfully saved 61,000 acres in southwest Broward from development with a building moratorium. As her political voice grew stronger, nevertheless, she lost three times in her bid to become the chair of the commission until finally, in 1980, she won the election unanimously. This was an historic first as well—the first woman chair of the County Commission of Broward. These were political moves in tandem with historic changes in the new environmental thrust she was pushing. She began negotiations with Federal officials to purchase the endangered mangrove swamp known as West Lake. The County Commission outdid itself when it passed the Urban Wilderness Park System, the only one of its kind in the country at that time. In 1978, the Florida Wildlife Federation named Anne Kolb Conservationist of the Year.

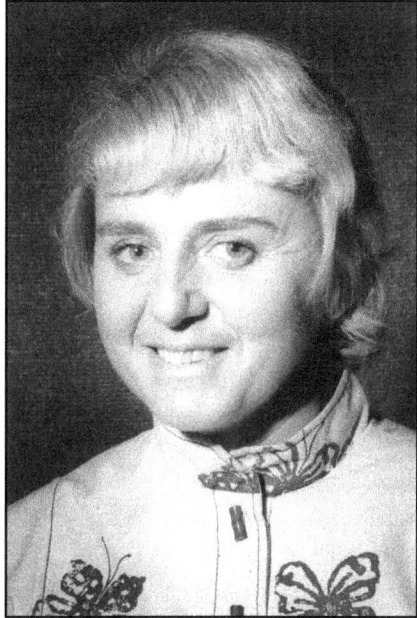

The press dubbed Anne Kolb Broward County's first lady.
Historical Commission archives

By this time, she was only three years from the end of her life as she began her valiant struggle with ovarian cancer. The County Commission rewarded her dedicated work for the environment when it named the West Lake nature park, the Anne Kolb Nature Park on June 2, 1981, just six weeks before she passed away.

One cannot read about Anne Kolb without feeling her passion for Florida and how she knew it so badly needed people to protect it from a disaster that, once done, could never be corrected. As a writer, a politician and an effective speaker, she projected the great anguish she felt about Florida's future. She rankled the commission staff when she challenged how and why they were spending taxpayers' money.

Not accustomed to anyone asking for sunshine in their work, they could not understand anyone who questioned them. And so when Anne Kolb stated, "The staff wants to run the government, and this has got to HALT", this was a great surprise. She felt it was her job as commissioner to be sure that taxpayers were being served well even if it meant she would be called a "meddler." In a 1969 story, she wrote, "Broward County's unplanned, multilayered government not only looks like the house that Jack built, it also functions like it." She quipped that Broward's cities were "money-making tools for the developers" and "the relationship between these cities and democracy is virtually nil." Her voice was shrill. Her passion was penetrating.

The Anne Kolb Nature Park at West Lake embodies her many faceted environmental concerns as a celebration of these concerns as well as a celebration of Anne Kolb as a great crusader of the Florida environment. Go visit.

The Anne Kolb Nature Center was named to honor her unflinching fight to save the environment.   Author's photo

Too Hot To Hide

Women's Firsts in Fort Lauderdale

Frankee Lewis (1745-1830) first matriarch of the first white American settlers in Fort Lauderdale, circa 1785.

Mary Brickell (1838-1922) "Single-handedly" responsible for the Florida East Coast Railway coming to Fort Lauderdale, 1896.

Ivy Stranahan (1881-1971)

　　Fort Lauderdale's first school teacher.

　　First woman on the Board of Managers, 1925.

　　First woman on the first Welfare Board, 1939.

　　Mother of Fort Lauderdale.

Fort Lauderdale Woman's Club (est. 1911)

　　Co-sponsored the first Seminole child to attend a white school, 1916.

　　Started the first library, 1916.

　　Started the first welfare board, 1939.

　　Started first Girl Scout troop, 1941.

Eva Oliver (1883-1964)

　　First president of the Fort Lauderdale Woman's Club, 1911.

　　First white woman married in Fort Lauderdale.

　　Town's first historian.

　　First woman to drive a car in town.

Annie Beck (1886-1985)

　　First to receive Florida Federation of Garden Clubs' Blanche Covington Award for outstanding leadership, 1945.

Annie Reed (1883-1955)

　　First president and founder of the Annie Reed Board, Mt. Hermon, AMC, 1910.

Annie Tommie (1856-1946)

　　First Seminole to allow her child a white education, 1916.

　　Led first group of Seminoles to their reservation, 1924.

Lorna Simpson (1908-1995)

　　One of two members of the WASP from Fort Lauderdale, 1940.

　　First Commercial Pilot Certificate, 1941.

　　First writer of a local children's TV show, "Pelican's Pouch."

Katherine Rawls (1918-1982)

First and only U.S. woman swimming competitor to win four Olympic events, 1936.

First woman in U.S. history to win four national championships in a single meet.

Named best woman athlete in U.S. by the Associated Press poll, 1937.

Fort Lauderdale's first national celebrity.

First woman to achieve Instructor Rating of the Commercial Certificate in aviation, 1941.

One of two members of the WASP from Fort Lauderdale, 1941.

Stella Taylor (1930-2003)

Oldest woman to swim the English Channel, 1972-75.

First and oldest woman to beat Lake George swim record, 1977.

Oldest woman to swim the Atlantic Ocean Gulf Stream, 1978.

Broke Guinness record of pool swimming, 1982.

Sylvia Aldridge (1884-1962)

First African-American woman entrepreneur, 1930.

Eula Johnson (1914-2001)

First woman president of NAACP, 1959-1967.

First black woman organizer of the historic "wade-in" at white beaches (as well as other demonstrations against segregation in Fort Lauderdale),1961.

Betty Mae Tiger Jumper (1923-2010)

First Seminole woman to attend a white school, ca.1938.

First Seminole interpreter at Jackson Memorial Hospital. 1945.

First Seminole health worker (known as Doctor Lady), 1947-1964.

First woman chair of the Tribal Council of Florida, 1966.

First founder of Southeastern Tribes, 1968.

Served two-year term as first woman member of National Tribal Council, 1970.

With Patsy West, wrote first book about Seminole culture.

Easter Lily Gates (1889-1985)

First woman school bus driver in Broward County.

First woman registrar of voters.

Registered first Seminoles and African-Americans to vote.

Too Hot To Hide

Florence Hardy (1897-1975)

> City auditor. 1927-1929.
> Assistant city manager. 1928.
> Acting Personnel Director. 1946-1951.
> First woman to receive the Woman of Achievement award 1954.
> Executive Assistant to City Commission. 1955.
>
> First woman who defined the post as county clerk and first woman to serve as county clerk, 1957.

Virginia Young (1897-1975)

> First woman mayor of Fort Lauderdale, 1973-75; 1981-1985.
>
> First woman to chair Board of Education.
>
> First woman elected president of Florida League of Cities.
>
> First woman director of a bank.

Kathleen Wright (1936-1985)

> First African-American woman elected to Board of Education, serving as chair or co-chair, 1973-1982.

Anne Kolb (1932-1981)

> First woman elected to the Broward County Board of Commissioners, 1974.
>
> First woman to chair the County Board of Commissioners, 1980.
>
> Broward county's first lady.

AFTERWORD

This narrative, while it speaks to remarkable women, also tells how their achievements connected with Fort Lauderdale and helped it to develop.

As I have read and reread this book, I cannot help but notice how often, if not always, I wrote about women who were volunteers. Many began as volunteers and stretched beyond. But many stretched into themselves as volunteers and began to grow into something else. That something else was usually—power. Volunteers tend to be women and as such are accustomed to "second class status." However, if one leans back and looks at what women do and can do, the word "power" can lead you to move aside from "second class status" into another world. The phrase, "just a volunteer," is a cop-out comment and shows no understanding of one's potential as a volunteer. This book should help turn one's head around regarding that misunderstanding.

I was most pleased to find Annie Reed and her Board at Mt. Hermon church. She was actually "hidden in history" until I learned about her just as her Board at the church celebrated its 100th anniversary of her founding it. While parts of her life existed in town, I took pleasure in discovering the pieces of her story and connecting them. Then when she and Ivy Stranahan conversed, so we think, in Ivy's Model T after Annie's workday, the need for land for the new colored school came up. So, we guess, Frank learned about that need from Ivy and he gave the land for Dillard School. However, I wanted to see the deed or the transaction whereby Frank Stranahan sold the Board of Education that land for $1.00, so the story goes in town. Neither the deed nor the transaction ever surfaced to validate that story. What surfaced was the letter from Ivy Stranahan who sold that land to the Board of Education for $10 in 1939. We should adjust that piece of town history.

Another part of town history needs amending. The plaque in Stranahan Park that reads "The Arrival of the Railroad 1896" contains a narrative that mentions Henry Flagler and Julia Tuttle. On that plaque, there is no mention of William and Mary Brickell who gave their Fort Lauderdale land to Flagler for the railroad depot and perhaps, more importantly, convinced him to include Fort Lauderdale on the Florida East Coast Railway's route. He was not too keen on the idea. Needless to say, the Brickell-Flagler railroad stop was vitally important to the commercial future of Fort Lauderdale in 1896. That leads me to a question: where would Fort Lauderdale be without the railroad? Mary Brickell is truly the unsung heroine in this railroad's history.

A piece of unfinished business is the Florence Hardy plaque given to her by her colleagues at city hall. A letter in her file stated that the plaque should be placed at the Fort Lauderdale Historical Society where she served after her retirement. At least, one can say the plaque is at the Society. It just isn't mounted. It sits in a drawer of the Society's Collections department. Whether it's at the Society or Hardy Park now undergoing expansion, it should be mounted where we can all appreciate her fine endeavors on behalf of the city.

Notice how often women worked together, regardless of color, to achieve an important event or change in town. Ivy worked with Annie Reed, with Annie Tommie and with Betty Mae Tiger Jumper. She became a member of the black Provident Hospital Board of Directors. Sylvia Aldridge became a "bridge" between the black and white Fort Lauderdale. Betty Mae Jumper Tiger and Annie Tommie served as bridges between the whites and the Seminoles in ways that profited both. Most of these activities were efforts by volunteers who behaved as partners in their quest for improvement among themselves and Fort Lauderdale.

Activities by volunteer groups such as the Fort Lauderdale Woman's Club showed brilliantly how volunteer efforts could and did craft parts of the city government in early Fort Lauderdale. The city library and welfare department began first inside the clubhouse and then outgrew that place into city governance. Some volunteers found themselves selected for membership on city boards. A subtle shift in the world of volunteers began. That shift would leave the volunteer sector with a requirement to...change.

The two champion women swimmers in this book stand on their own as sparkling ambassadors, celebrities of Fort Lauderdale. Katy Rawls' involvement in the evolution of the College Forum and the Casino Pool into the International Swimming Hall of Fame stands tall in history. This happened as Fort Lauderdale faced a question about its definition, its persona. Stella Taylor, a swimming star almost at the other end of the age spectrum compared to Katy Rawls, swam with courage and determination. Her spectacular, daring marathon swimming feats defied our usual expectations about older women who were swimmers. Both these swimmers made international headlines and when they did, so did Fort Lauderdale. Obviously, such press coverage boosted Fort Lauderdale's stature in the world and in swimming.

As the status of women and African-Americans advanced after their WWII work experiences demonstrated how competent they could be in the workforce where they had never been before, that status did not relegate them back to the pre-WWII place. It was a jump that showed the way to the Civil Rights and women's movement in the 1960s and '70s. Actually, it was a leap. Both "minorities," women and the African-Americans, began to move out of the second-class, home or volunteer sector into government service. They began to run for political office, a paid job that was competitive to achieve.

Perhaps the best example of that change can be seen in Mayor Virginia Young's life story. As a member of just about every volunteer organization in town, she felt groomed enough to run for Mayor. She did not win every election, but won enough to give her the Mayor's post two times, non-consecutively. Since then, many women have run for various commissions, boards, etc. of the town. She, however, has never been trumped as mayor. She is still our one and only woman mayor as of this writing.

Evelyn Bartlett's strides into the preservation of her Bonnet House and its grounds in perpetuity were unusual. We actually do not know how many times commercial developers tried to convince her to sell her place. She stood fast and left Fort Lauderdale a piece of early Florida impossible to replicate today.

I believe that women inherently are the conscience of the community they live in. When they organize, that collective conscience can be very powerful. They want to change what's wrong into what's right and complete any omissions. Historically, when allowed by society and permitted by law, this is what women do. Each woman has a talent, a skill, a vision to inject into a community. Some suggest it is a right and a responsibility to exercise these injections.

The best example of a powerful woman who recognized her potential was Eula Johnson. As the first woman president of the National Association for the Advancement of Colored People in town, she honed enough organizing skills to lead boycotts and demonstrations to correct segregation in town. Her pressure was unrelenting. Her attitude was brave and bold. She used the law to change the status quo in town. As her grandson said on July 4, 2011, in front of his grandmother's house, "My grandmother sued everybody in town." The audience laughed, knowingly.

The women in this book were women with outstanding or unusual abilities. Often, they were brave in facing danger. They knew how to use their abilities to improve Fort Lauderdale. Deep-down, they knew they had achieved power and learned how to flex that power for improvement in town. Each of these women was a star, often when more darkness than sun surrounded them.

Too Hot To Hide

SOURCES

To find **the Lewis family** anywhere was practically impossible. Patrick Scott's article about them is the closest one can get to who they were. But there is very little about Frankee Pickett Lewis. Harold Flagg's article brought this family to life, however. As loyalists leaving the colonies after the Revolutionary War, they were impossible to track. No lists of loyalists from any of the 13 colonies exist. So to find exactly which colony they came from is not possible. Where exactly the Lewises settled in Abaco is also not possible. If any lists of the loyalists do exist it is likely they are in England. My trip to the Bahamas Archives did not bring up any information I could use. Another reason for the Lewis' anonymity was their vocation. They were "only farmers." Lists of "important people" like lawyers, boat-builders, preachers, doctors, etc. exist, but not lowly farmers. Only recently Chris Barfield, Collections Manager of the Fort Lauderdale Historical Society, discovered the Lewis family via Ancestry.com. Many thanks to Chris for finding some unknown information about Frankee.

The coontie plant was most interesting to discover. Its part in defining southeast Florida's first industry, its transfer process from the Seminoles to the white Americans struck me as fascinating. Around the same time that I was writing this book, the Woman's Club included the coontie plant in their new Butterfly Garden. I also included it in my Women's History Walk.

Abraham, Randy. "Fort Lauderdale Dedicates Coontie Hatche Park in Riverside Area." *Sun Sentinel* 13, 2009.

Burkhardt, Mrs. Henry. "Starch Making, A Pioneer Florida Industry."*Tequesta*. No. xii, 1952.

Crary, Catherine S. *The Price of Loyalty*. McGraw-Hill, NY, 1973.

Dodge, Steve. *Abaco*. White Sound Press, Florida, 2005.

Flagg, Harold. "Bahamian Lewises: Pioneers of Florida." *Bahamas Handbook*, Etienne Dupuch, Jr. Publications, Nassau, 1997.

Gaby, Donald C. "The Early Years Upriver." *Tequesta*. No. xlviii, 1988.

Gearhart, Ernest C., Jr. "South Florida's First Industry." *Tequesta*. No. xii, 1952.

George, Paul S. *A Jewel in the Wilderness. Fort Lauderdale from Early Times to 1911*. Broward County Comprehensive Survey. Phase viii. May 1988.

Gifford, John C. "Five Plants Essential to the Indians and Early Settlers of Florida." *Tequesta*. No. 4. Nov. 1944.

Knetsch, Joe. *Florida's Seminole Wars. 1817-1858*. Arcadia Press, SC, 2003.

Peters, Thelma. "The American Loyalists in the Bahamas: Who They Were." *Florida Historical Quarterly*. Vol. 40, Jan. 1962.

_____. "The Loyalist Migration from East Florida to the Bahama Islands." *Florida Historical Quarterly*. Oct. 1961.

Scott, Patrick. "The Many Heirs of Jonathan Lewis." *Broward Legacy*. Summer/ Fall, 1994.

Siebert, Wilbur. H. *Loyalists in East Florida. 1774-1785*. Delano Historical Society, 1929.

There are many books about the 41 years of the Seminole Wars. I confess a real prejudice about listing them all because I did not read them all. Joe Knetsch's *Florida's Seminole Wars, 1817-1858* helped me understand the reasons for these wars. I must make another confession, and that is I feel most war books are all the same. Strategies and examples of victories are not what turn me on. Joe's book gives a good bibliography of the war books.

The story of **Mary Brickell** made me an instant fan. How she managed, how she convinced, how she "arm twisted" Henry Flagler into stopping his railroad in Fort Lauderdale was a great discovery and a delightful story. Beth Brickell's book certainly documented Mary's role in bringing the railroad to town. In doing so, Mary served Fort Lauderdale business community extremely well and helped the town to grow.

Brickell, Beth. *William and Mary Brickell*. History Press, Charleston, SC, 2011. The files at the Hoch Center of the Fort Lauderdale Historical Society and the Broward County Historical Commission contained many articles including the two articles I used:

"Colored People Mourn Mrs. Brickell's Passing." *Miami Herald*. Jan 14, 1922.

"Mrs. Mary Brickell Died Suddenly at 12.40 this Morning." *Miami Herald*. Jan. 13, 1922.

There is no shortage of information about **Ivy Stranahan**. Many thanks to Merrilyn Rathbun, Research Director, Hoch Center of the Fort Lauderdale Historical Society. The files used here are available at the Hoch Center.

Burghard, August and Weidling, Philip. *Checkered Sunshine*. Wake-Brook House. Fort Lauderdale Historical Society, 1974.

Burghard, August. *Watchie-Esta-Hutrie*. Fort Lauderdale Historical Society, 1968.

Cassels, Alice Cromartie, Dinerman, Barbara Jones, Rosemary E. and McIver Stuart. *Stranahan House*. Stranahan Historical Society, 1995.

Kersey, Harry A. Jr. *The Stranahans of Fort Lauderdale*. University Press of Florida, Miami, 2003.

Information about the **Fort Lauderdale Woman's Club** exists in an archival form in its minutes kept at the Broward County Historical Commission. These minutes show the lively involved club through the years from its beginning in 1911 to the present time. Other information comes from these sources. The files are at the Hoch Center, Fort Lauderdale Historical Society library.

Houde, Mary Jean. *Reaching Out: A Story of the Federal Federation of Women's Clubs*. Mobium Press, Chicago, 1989.

"Thumbnail Sketch of our History—1911", unknown author.

Vreeland, Cordelia D. "The First Years of the Fort Lauderdale Woman's Club." *Broward Legacy*, Summer/Fall, 1990.

History about **Eva Oliver** exists mostly in the files at the Hoch Center of the Fort Lauderdale Historical Society. Merrilyn Rathbun, Research Director and Chris Barfield, Curator of collections are both quite knowledgeable and helpful.

These files were very helpful about **Annie Beck** also. However, Ann Schandelmayer, president emeritus of the Fort Lauderdale Garden Club, knew Annie Beck, wrote a very good article about her, and spoke to me about her. She sent me the photograph of *Tababuia Argenta* and its historic move from its place at Annie Beck's front yard to the new place in Middle River Terrace Park. Inside the Garden Clubhouse in Birch Park, is Annie Beck's library which she donated years ago. Annie Beck's house, recently restored, is now ready for occupancy as it sits proudly in Middle River Terrace Park.

Files at Fort Lauderdale Historical Society, Hoch Center.

Burkhard, August. *Half a Century in Florida*. Manatee Books, Fort Lauderdale, 1966.

Schandelmayer, Ann. "Farewell to a Great Lady," *The Florida Gardener*. May/June, 1985.

The unknown **Annie Reed** story, as it unfolded, was fascinating. In an interview with Mrs. Ellyn Walters, who lived with Annie Reed while she attended Dillard School, gave me much insight into this remarkable woman. Her advice sent me to the Mt. Hermon Church to meet Annie Reed's Board. Mrs. Jackson, current president of Annie's Board, gave me a copy of her tribute to Annie Reed that she gave on the day the church celebrated the centennial of Annie's Board. I met the present Board and took their picture.

Broward County Board of Education School Records. Book 2, pp. 548-49.

Celebration Report as read by Mrs. N. Jackson, August 23, 2009 at the Mt. Hermon AME Church.

Work, Deborah. *My Soul is Witness. A History of Black Fort Lauderdale*. Donning Co Publishers, Virginia Beach, VA, 2001.

Interview with Mrs. Ellyn Ferguson Walters. Aug. 10, 2009.

Special thanks to Kala Luzia, Special. Collections Librarian, African-American Library and Museum; and Jonathan Peservich, Delores Burrell at the Broward County Board of Education: .

The information about **Annie Tommie** was found in the files at Hoch Center, Fort Lauderdale Historical Society.

Covington, James. W. *The Seminoles of Florida*. University Press of Florida, 1992.

Kersey, Harry A. Jr. *The Florida Seminoles and the New Deal*. Florida Atlantic Univ. Press, Boca, Raton, 1989.

_____ *The Stranahans of Fort Lauderdale*. Univ. Press of Florida.

West, Patsy. *The Seminoles and Miccoosukee Tribes of Southern Florida*. Arcadia Press. Charleston,SC, 2002.

Too Hot To Hide

Information about **Lorna Simpson** is scant. The files at the Hoch Center of the Fort Lauderdale Historical Society contain copies of the one and only picture I've found of Lorna. *The Evening Sentinel*, Sunday, June 21, 1941 has a lovely picture of Lorna which is in this book. Lorna also wrote a five-page *History of Aviation in Fort Lauderdale* which is in the files. Requests to the WASP collections at Texas Women's University, Denton, Texas for her picture have not been successful. Copies of Lorna's "Pelican's Pouch" radio scripts are at the Broward County Historical Commission.

The WAFS, Women's Auxiliary Flying Squadron, morphed into the WASP, Women's Airforce Service Pilots, in 1943 and deactivated in 1944. Two places in Texas hold collections, memorabilia about WASP: Denton and Sweetwater which includes Avenger Field, the largest women's airfield in the United States. The National WASP WWII Museum resides at Sweetwater. The Internet contains much information about these two sites. Women in WASP waited for 34 years before their duty was legitimized by our government. In 1977 the Senate granted WASP members veteran status. President Carter made the Senate's grant official a few months later.

Many articles exist about **Katy Rawls** at the Hoch Center, Fort Lauderdale Historical Society. Many can also be found at the Henning Library of the International Swimming Hall of Fame. Her memorabilia is also at Henning as well as a exhibit of her life at the Museum. Special thanks to Robert Dunckel, Curator and Executive Director of the International Swimming Hall of Fame; to Marion Washburn, Librarian at the Henning Library, ISHF; and to Merrilyn Rathbun, Research Director, Hoch Center of the Fort Lauderdale Historical Society. The bulk of my research material came from the files at the Henning Library and Hoch Center library.

Cosco, Joseph. "Champion Swimmer Katy Rawls Dies." *Fort Lauderdale News*, April 9, 1982. 1B.

Cox, Susan. "Swimmer Packs Olympic Memories." *Fort Lauderdale News*, December 29, 1973.

Burghard, August. *Half a Century in Florida*. Manatee Books, Fort Lauderdale, 1982.

Dawson, Buck. *Weismuller to Spitz. International Swimming Hall of Fame.* 1987.

_____. *Why Fort Lauderdale?* five-page pamphlet, n.d.

Randle, Nancy Jalasca. "When Fly Girls Soared" *Sun Sentinel, May 24, 1999.* 3D.

Material about **Stella Taylor** came mostly from the Henning Library at the International Swimming Hall of Fame.

Cheslow, Steve. *Knickerbocker News*, front page, June 8, 1977.

Williams, Kathy. "Stella the Woman-Child", *Evening Times*, April 15, 1981.

Special thanks to librarian Marion Washburn at the Henning Library; Robert Dunckle, Executive Director of the International Swimming Hall of Fame; and Clarise Knowles-Rousseau at the Lauderdale Memorial Cemetery.

Sources of information about **Sylvia Aldridge** were in two books.

Black Pioneers in Broward County. Published by the Links. 1976.

Work, Deborah. *My Soul is a Witness*. Donning Co. Publishers, VA, 2001.

These two books were central in my research about local black history. The unraveling of the second-class status of women, African-Americans, and gays occurred during WWII, and their movements began to flower after the war. I looked at the local as well as national shifts to reveal these changes in our society and culture. For the local history, Susan Gillis in her *Fort Lauderdale, The Venice of America* (Arcadia Press, Charleston, SC, 2004) gives an excellent panoramic focus of the town. Matching that with Kristin Andersen's *Port Everglades, A Century of Opportunity* (published by Port Everglades of Broward County, 2000), given to me by Port staff member Andy Deering, shows the interplay of the port with the history of the town during wartime. For the women's work during the war and afterwards, I used Philip Foner's *Women and the American Labor Movement*, (The Free Press, NY, 1982) and *America's Working Women*, compiled and edited by Rosalyn Baxandall, Linda Gordon and Susan Reverby (Vintage Books, NY, 1976). The African-American desegregation story is from Deborah Work's *My Soul is a Witness*. op. cit.

Eula Johnson's story and her campaign to turn Fort Lauderdale upside down were easily followed in the newspaper clippings at the Hoch Center of the Fort Lauderdale Historical Society. These articles were especially helpful.

Davis, Gerald." Civil Rights Crusader helped forge new freedoms," *Miami Herald*, February 2, 1988.

DeMarzo, Wanda J. and Berrios, Jerry. "Civil Rights Pioneer," *Miami Herald*, January 21, 2001.

Personal notes from July 4, 2011 event at Mrs. Johnson's home.

Black Pioneers in Broward County. Published by the Links, 1976.

Work, Deborah. *My Soul is a Witness*. pp. 138-48.

Betty Mae Tiger Jumper had a wonderful collaborator, Patsy West, who knew about native Americans first hand. Through the eyes of both these outstanding women, the remarkable Dr. Jumper came to life for me. Both of these sources will bring her triumphant story to you.

Jumper, Betty Mae Tiger and West, Patsy. *A Seminole Legend*. University Press of Florida, Gainesville, FL, 2001.

West, Patsy. "Seminole Activist", *Making Waves*, ed. Davis, Jack E. and Frederickson, Kari, University Press of Florida, 2003, pp. 56-73.

Information about **Easter Lily Gates** came from a transcribed interview with Mrs. Gates: "Pioneer Woman Politician: An Oral Interview with Easter Lily Gates" conducted by Cooper Kirk, Phd. and transcribed and edited by Carolyn G. Kayne. *Broward Legacy*, Vol 5, Summer/Fall, 1982. pp. 18-39.

Sources for information about **Florence Hardy** and **Virginia Young** came from files at the Hoch Center, Fort Lauderdale Historical Society. Virginia Shuman Young tells you her story in her book, *Mangrove Roots of Fort Lauderdale*. (Poinsettia Press, 1961).

Information about the preservation movement came from the lively written book, *Keeping Time* by William Murtach (Sterling Publishing, NY, 1993). For information bout **Evelyn Bartlett**, I owe special thanks to Noell Shuey Altamirano, Curator at Bonnet House, who provided files and the Smithsonian video for me to view.

Oliver, Kitty. *African Amerians Remember Bonnet House,* 1999.

Rice, Jayne Thomas. *Bonnet House: The Life and Gift*. Bonnet House, 1990.

Files at the Hoch Center, Fort Lauderdale Historical Society.

The life of **Kathleen Wright** is well documented in numerous newspaper clippings about her career as an educator. Her voice, however, shines true in the minutes of the Broward County Board of Education meetings.

"Ex-Official is Honored by Schools." *Miami Herald,* February 18,1987.

Gerety, Justine. "Friends Bid Farewell to Kathleen Wright." *Sun Sentinel,* September 1, 1985.

"Tribute to Educator takes Shape." *Miami Herald,* March 30, 1998.

Work, Deborah. *My Soul is a Witness*. Donning Co. Publishers, Virginia Beach, VA, 2001.

Board of Education Minutes. Books 32-45. Special thanks to Renata Turcios and Niemi Gutierrez for their assistance regarding this material.

Anne Kolb's life can almost be best understood when one visits the nature reserve named for her. While staff there hardly knew much about her, I felt her distinct presence in that place. Sources about her come from newspaper clippings at the Hoch Center, Fort Lauderdale Historical Society.

Cibert, Al. "In Florida." *Miami Herald,* March 2, 1980. *Broward News,* July 27,1981

I must comment about how helpful the newspaper clipping files are at the Hoch Center of the Fort Lauderdale Historical Society. One might think this comment obvious. Isn't this what libraries are supposed to have? One would be surprised how many libraries do not have good newspaper clipping files. Since Fort Lauderdale history is not long in years, the information in newspapers is quite valuable and sometimes the only source of information available about some of the women in this book. I extend special thanks to their newspaper clipping staff.

The clipping files were especially important since very little, if any, autobiographical information is available about these women. There are few letters, and no diaries exist. There are some "howevers" to his statement. Virginia Young's book written with the help of Gretchen Thompson is the closest that one can find to a diary about her life. Eva Oliver's written historical articles can easily be considered her diary. The book of Dr. Jumper's life story stands as a diary. Ivy Stranahan, the town's first school teacher, left no diary. However, oral histories of many of these women exist and are transcribed. These are valuable.

FOOTNOTES

1.   Brickell, Beth. *William and Mary Brickell*. p. 73. li.

2.   Ibid. p. 91.

3.   Ibid. p, 67.

4.   Ibid. pp.73-76.

5.   Houde, Mary Jean. *Reaching Out: A History of the Federal Federation of Women's Clubs*. Mobium Press, Chicago, 1989. p. 156.

6.   Ibid. p. 153.

7.   Ibid. p. 322.

8.   Washburn, Beatrice. "Don't Resign from Active Life." *Miami Herald*. n.d.

9.   Ibid.

10,   *Broward County Board of Education School Records*. Book 2, pp. 548-49

11.   Simpson, Lorna. *History of Aviation in Fort Lauderdale*. Typewritten. 5 p. n.d. pg. 1.

12.   Dawson, Buck. *Weiszmuller to Spitz. International Swimming Hall of Fame*, 1987. p. 230.

13.   Work Deborah. *My Soul is a Witness*. Donning Co. Publishers, Virginia Beach, VA, 2000, p 38.

14.   Kirk, Cooper, oral interviewer. Kayne, Carolyn G., editor. "An Oral Interview with Easter Lily Gates." *Broward Legacy*. Vol. 5. Summer/Fall, 1982. pp. 18-39. p33.

15.   *Ibid*. all quotes from pp. 35-36.

16.   Young, Virginia. *Mangrove Roots of Fort Lauderdale*. Poinsettia Press, 1961. p. 14. All subsequent quotations from pp. 36-47.

Index

Author's Biography

Mae Kramer Silver has been writing local history for more than two decades. She began writing in San Francisco when she discovered the land her house sat on was part of a Mexican rancho. It became intriguing to write local history stories that no one else had written. Before she wrote about her neighborhood, she discovered a story about historic *Trolley 130* which had been saved from demolition by a "guardian angel" who worked in the public railway system. Her neighborhood history stretched into stories about all the current neighborhoods that were previously in Rancho San Miguel. That book became a slideshow which she took into the Rancho neighborhoods. Turning to the world of women's history, she wrote *The Sixth Star* which chronicled the two campaigns the suffragists mounted in California to secure a state constitutional amendment that gave them the right to vote. In between these books, she wrote many articles for journals and newspapers.

Mae is also a community organizer. She founded her neighborhood association first called Twin Peaks East, now renamed Corbett Street Neighbors. She sat on the founding board of the San Francisco Historical Society, now called the San Francisco Museum and Historical Society. She served as president of the San Francisco History Association, vice-president of the National Council of Jewish Women and was appointed by Superintendent Cortines as chair of the Library Media Committee of the San Francisco School district. As parliamentarian, she served the San Francisco Coalition of Neighborhoods. When she returned to her home state of New Jersey in 2003, she settled in Bordentown to tap into her roots and to write about the famous Thomas Paine who lived intermittently in Bordentown during the Revolutionary times. There she founded the Thomas Paine Society of Bordentown, Inc. and created a monthly walk "In the Footsteps of Thomas Paine". That tour became a book with the name *In His Footsteps: Finding Thomas Paine in Bordentown, New Jersey*. In addition, she wrote *Messenger to the World* for the New Jersey Press Foundation publication to all the New Jersey newspapers. She also wrote a keepsake for the Thomas Paine Society called *Thomas Paine's Christmas Bridge*. To explore the beauty of Bordentown's outside wrought iron ornamentation, she wrote *Iron Lace*.

In 2008, when she moved to Fort Lauderdale to be near her daughter Judith, she continued to write local history and produced *Watch Out, Ivy*. *Too Hot to Hide* is an offshoot of her women's history walk (of the same name) that she leads once a month. *Too Hot to Hide* is Mae's ninth book.

www.toohottohide.com

Acknowledgements

I gave my manuscript to many in the community. Some made corrections and comments and with others I had interesting discussions. I wish to thank Maggie Davidson, President of the Democratic Women's Club of Northeast Broward; Mrs. Helen Landers, Broward County Historian; Will Trower, Executive Director of the Fort Lauderdale Historical Society; Patsy West, ethnohistorian of the Seminoles; Robert Cannon, Director of the Broward County Libraries; and Susan Gills, historian and history director of the Fort Lauderdale Centennial Celebration, 2011. Any errors in the text are mine alone. Alan K. Lipton of Berkeley, California, gave this book a wonderful edit. Writing *Too Hot to Hide* was only one part of this production. The craft of creating this book lies in the able hands and mind of Chris Carlsson from San Francisco. My great thanks to him.

www.ingramcontent.com/pod-product-compliance
Lightning Source LLC
Chambersburg PA
CBHW052106090426
42741CB00009B/1695